Spanish Phrases for Landscaping Professionals

Jason Holben and Dominic Arbini

Stock Pot Publishing
P.O. Box 18343
Denver, CO 80218-0343

ISBN 0-9659717-1-6

Written by Jason B. Holben and
Dominic Arbini

Translations by Veronica Horn and
Pedro Petit

Layout and Design by

Majordomo's® Inc.
1155 Sherman St., Suite 210
Denver, CO 80203

Thanks to Scott Jenkins at Bayou City Backyards in Spring, TX for giving this book a trial run. To Veronica Horn for her patience and accuracy. To Pedro Petit for his guidance through slang and regional dialects....and especially to all of the Hispanic crews that we have worked with. We would have been out of business if it weren't for your efforts and skill.

After sixteen years of combined landscaping experience; from running mowers to running crews, we have found that a working understanding of the Spanish language is priceless... we've also found that learning Spanish from textbooks after a 60 hour week is impossible.

You will find this book easy to use and extremely helpful in all facets of Landscaping from hiring and training to maintaining quality and consistency throughout. All of the 1600+ words and phrases presented here have been translated from both an academic and a "street" perspective.

Just as the English language has many dialects and twangs, so too does the Spanish language. The translations provided here and the way that your staff may prefer to pronounce them are likely to differ slightly from time to time. When this happens, it is our sincere hope that y'all get a good laugh out of it, and a better understanding of what is being said.

We have intentionally left a few blank pages at the end of each section so that you can customize this book with phrases, words and special services that are specific to your operation.

CONTENTS

School

A Crash Course in Spanish.

This section covers the **very** basics of Spanish Grammar. You **will** be understood if you use this book without ever looking at this section. However, by going over these few rules, your ability to speak and understand Spanish will come to you more quickly, and more easily.

Pronunciation

Vowels: For good pronunciation in Spanish, focus on the vowels. One vowel sound pronounced incorrectly can change the meaning of a word entirely. In Spanish, there is only one sound for each vowel, whereas in English there are several. If you can pronounce these five (5) sounds clearly and correctly, you will avoid being misunderstood.

A - Always pronounced like the "A" in Father.
E - Always pronounced like the "A" in Make.
I - Always pronounced like a "Double E" in See.
O - Always pronounced like the "O" in So.
U - Always pronounced like a "Double O" in Moo.

Consonants: (Letters other than A, E, I, O, U)

C - Pronounced like the English 'K' when it is before 'A', O and 'U'or another consonant. Before 'I' or 'E', it is pronounced like the English 'S'.

- If you have 2 'C's back to back, the first is pronounced like 'K', and the second like 'S'.

i.e. Dirección (Direk-sion)

- A 'C' followed by an 'H' is pronounced just like it is in English.

i.e. Chico (Chee-co)

G - Pronounced like the English 'G' in Go when it is followed by 'A', 'O', 'U' or another consonant.

- When followed by 'E' or 'I', it is pronounced like a strongly aspirated English H as in House or Ha.
- The ''U in 'UE' and 'UI' is silent after 'G' and makes the 'G' hard,, as in guest.

H - Is always silent (except after 'C', in which case it sounds like 'CH' in English.)

J - Is pronounced like a strongly aspirated English 'H' as in House or Ha.

LL - Is pronounced like the English 'Y' as in Yolk.

Ñ - Is pronounced like the English letter combination of 'N' and 'Y' as in Canyon or Kenya.

Q - Is pronounced like the English 'K'. It is always followed by 'UE' or 'UI', as the 'U' is always silent. i.e. Que = 'K" and Quien = Key-n.

R - Is strongly trilled in Spanish. This is difficult for many non-native Spanish (or Italian) speakers. If you can't trill your tongue, try saying words with a double 'D', such as Eddie. The 'DD' gives the closest imitation to the tongue movement and sound of the Spanish R.

RR - Double 'R' is a noticeably longer version of the Single 'R'. There are words whose meanings change with the difference of these letters. i.e. Carro = car and Caro = expensive. Don't worry too much if you are unable to trill your 'R's, or stretch your 'RR's. You will be understood 99% of the time through the context of the sentence and / or the setting you are in.

V - Is pronounced like the English 'B'.

X - Is pronounced like the English 'X' in Examine or Exact. In the words Mexico and Mexicano, it is pronounced as if it were a Spanish 'J' (for the former spelling Méjico and Mejicano)

Y - Is usually pronounced like the English 'Y' in Young; when it stands alone or is followed by a vowel, it is pronounced like the double 'E' in See. For example:

hoy	pronounced 'oee'
muy	pronounced 'mooee'
voy	pronounced 'boee'
ay	pronounced 'ie'
y	pronounced 'ee'

Z - Is pronounced like the English 'S'.

- Letters and variations of letters not mentioned are either pronounced exactly like their English counterparts or the differences are slight and will not cause any major misunderstanding.

* **Accents** are a vast and complex study. Be sure to emphasize written accents. Unwritten emphasis within words and best learned by listening and repeating.

- **Phonetics** - The phonetics (pronunciations) provided in this book were written by a gringo (American) for Gringos. They are neither academic nor 'official', but they are accurate.

- **Articles (The's)** Always agree with nouns (person, place or thing), in both gender (masculine/ feminine) and number (singular or plural). Therefore there are four (4) forms of the word 'the'.

  El - Masculine Singular - El libro
  Los - Masculine Plural - Los Libros
  La - Feminine Singular - La Casa
  Las - Feminine Plural - Las Casas

- **Adjectives -** (Describes a noun): Must agree with nouns and articles in both gender and number.

  El libro rojo
  Los Libros Rojos
  La Casa Grande
  Las Casas Grandes

  * In English, the adjective preceds the noun. ie: The Red Book.
  * In Spanish, they follow the noun. ie: The Book Red (El libro rojo)

- **Verbs** (Describes Actions): Proper Spanish verb usage is infinitely complex and conditional. For the purposes of this book, some have been conjugated, some have not. They are in the form that most simplifies and facilitates their use in given context.

Common Sentence Leads

Who	Quién...	*(Key-n)*
What	Qué ...	*(K)*
When	Cuándo ...	*(Kwan-doe)*
Where	Dónde ...	*(Dohn-day)*
Why	Por Qué ...	*(Poor-k)*
How	Cómo	*(Co-moe)*
Because	Porque (one word, no accent)	*(Porkay)*
Do you have	Tienes	*(T-n-ehs)*
Do you need	Necesitas	*(Neh-seh-c-tahs)*
Do we have	Tenemos	*(Teh-neh-mose)*
I have	Tengo	*(Tehn-go)*
I need	Necesito	*(Neh-seh-c-toe)*
... this	Esto	*(S-toe)*
... that	Eso	*(S-oh)*
Where is	Dónde está	*(Dohn-day s-tah)*
Where are	Dónde están	*(Dohn-day s-tahn)*
Do you know	Sabes	*(Sah-bays)*
I don't know	No sé	*(No-say)*
I	Yo	*(Yo)*

You	Tú	*(Too)*
He	Él	*(El)*
She	Ella	*(A-yah)*
We	Nosotros	*(No-sow-trohs)*
Y'all	Ustedes	*(Ooh-steh-dehs)*
They (men)	Ellos	*(A-yohs)*
They (women)	Ellas	*(A-yahs)*
My (singular)	Mi	*(Me)*
My (plural)	Mis	*(Meese)*
Yours (singular)	Tu	*(Too)*
Yours (plural)	Tus	*(Toohs)*
His / Hers (singular)	Su	*(Soo)*
His / Hers (plural)	Sus	*(Soohs)*
Ours (singular)	Nuestro	*(Nway-strow)*
Ours (plural)	Nuestros	*(Nway-strows)*
Theirs (singular)	Su	*(Soo)*
Theirs (plural)	Sus	*(Soohs)*

Notes
Apuntes
(Ah-poon-tehs)

How do you say _______________ in Spanish ?
Cómo se dice _______________ en Español?
(Koe-moe say d-say __________ en s-pahn-yohl?)

Notes
Apuntes
(Ah-poon-tehs)

How do you say _______________ in Spanish ?
Cómo se dice _______________ en Español?
(Koe-moe say d-say __________ en s-pahn-yohl?)

You're Hired!

Getting people in the door, documented and familiar with the basic do's and don'ts of your operation.

Hello
Hola
(Oh-la)

My name is ...
Yo me llamo es...
(Yo-may yam-mo es...)

What is your name?
Cómo te llamas?
(Koe-moe tay yam-mas?)

Do you speak any english?
Tu hablas ingles?
(too ahb-lahs een-glace)

Do you have landscaping experience?
Tienes experiencia en ajardinar?
(T-N-ehs x-peer-n-c-ah N ah-har-deen-ahr?)

I need full / part time help.
Yo necesito ***tiempo completo / tiempo parcial.***
(yoh neh-ceh-c-toh T-M-poh cohm-play-toh / t-m-poe par-c-ahl)

Can you work days?
Puedes trabajar días?
(Puay-thays tra-bah-har dee-ahs)

Can you work nights?
Puedes trabajar noches?
(Puay-thays tra-bah-har no-chays)

Can you be here early (at 6:00)?
Puedes estar aqui temprano (a la seis)?
(pway-thays s-tahr ah-key tehm-prah-noh (ah la sase))

Can you work Saturdays and / or Sundays?
Trabajarias Sabados y / o domingos?
(trah-bah-har-e-ahs Sah-bah-thos E / O doh-ming-gohs)

It is necessary to work weekends.
Es necesario trabajar los fines de semana.
(S neh-seh-sar-e-o traj-bah-har lohs fee-nehs day seh-mah-nah)

Are you willing to work more than (40) hours per week?
Esta dispuesto a trabajar mas de (cuarenta) horas por semana?
(s-tah dihs-pwehs-toh ah trah-bah-har mahs day (kwar-n-tah) or-ahs pohr seh-mah-nah)

You are only permitted to work (40) hours per week.
Tu puedes trabajar solamente (quarenta) horas por semana?
(to pway-thays trah-bah-har so-lah-mehn-tay(kwar-n-tah) or-ahs pohr seh-mah-nah)

Using drugs or alcohol on the job is prohibited.
El uso de drogas o alcohol en el trabajo es prohibido.
(L ooh-soh day droh-gahs Oh ahl-coh-holl N L trah-bah-hoe S pro-he-b-doh)

If you are hung over, drunk or stoned I will send you home.
Si vienes cruda o borracho o drogado te mando a tu casa.
(C B-n-ehs croo-tha Oh bor-ratch-o Oh drow-gah-tho, tay mahn-doh ah too cah-sah)

If you are late more than (3) times you are fired.
Si llegas tarde mas de (tres) veces tu serás despedido.
(C yay-gahs tahr-day mahs day (trace) beh-sehs too seh-rahs dehs-peh-d-doh)

Do you understand?
Tu entiendes?
(too N-T-N-dehs)

The job is dangerous / demanding.
El trabajo es peligroso/exigente.
(L trah-bah-hoe S pehl-e-groh-soh / X-E-hen-tay)

This job requires heavy lifting.
Este trabajo requiere levantar objectos pesados.
(s-tay trah-bah-hoe reh-kweh-ray leh-bahn-tahr ohb-hect-ohs peh-sah-dohs)

This job requires a lot of overtime.
Este trabajo requiere trabajar horas extras.
(s-tay trah-bah-hoe reh-kweh-reh trah-bah-har or-ahs x-trahs)

You will be working in all kinds of weather.
Tu estaras trabajando en toda clase de tiempo.
(2 s-tahr-ahs trah-bah-han-doh N toh-dah clah-say day T-M-poe)

This is seasonal work.
Este es un trabajo temporal.
(s-tay S oohn trah-bah-hoe tehm-poh-rahl)

This job ends in the fall.
Este trabajo termina en el otoño
(s-tay trah-bah-hoe tehr-me-nah N L oh-tone-yoh)

We hire again in the spring.
Nosotros contratamos otra vez en la primavera.
(noh-so-trohs cohn-tra-tah-mohs oh-tra behs N la pre-mah-behr-ah)

You must have a drivers license.
Tu tienes que tener licencia para manejar.
(2 T-N-ehs K teh-nair lee-sin-c-ah pah-rah mah-nay-har)

We don't offer health insurance.
Nosotros no ofrecemos seguro de salud.
(no-soh-trohs no oh-fray-say-mohs seh-goo-roh day sah-lood)

We offer health insurance after (6) months.
Nosotros ofrecemos seguro de salud despues de seis meses.
(noh-soh-trohs oh-fray-say-mohs seh-goo-roh dehs-puehs day sayce meh-sehs)

Fill out these forms.
Llena estos formularios.
(yeah-nah s-toes for-moo-lar-e-ohs.)

Application
Aplicación / Solicitud
(Ahp-le-kah-see-ohn / So-liss-e-tude)

Resumé
Resumen / currículum.
(Reh-soo-mehn / coor-ree-coo-luhm)

Do you have references?
Tienes referencias?
(T-N-ehs ref-er-in-c-ahs?)

Name
Nombre
(Nome-bray)

Address
Dirección
(D-rek-see-ohn)

Telephone Number
Número de teléfono
(Noo-mer-o day tel-eh-foe-no)

When is a good time to call?
Cuándo es conveniente llamarte?
(Quan-doe s con-ben-e-en-tay yam-mar-teh?)

How will you get here?
Cómo vas a llegar aquí?
(Koe-moe bahs ah yea-gar ah-key?)

When can you start?
Cuándo puedes empezar?
(Quan-doe pway-thays emp-eh-sahr?)

Today
Hoy
(Oy)

Tomorrow
Mañana
(Mahn-yahn-ah)

In (5) Days.
En (cinco) Días
(N (seen-coh) Dee-ahs)

Monday.
Lunes
(loo-nehs)

I'll let you know.
Te diré pronto.
(Tay d-ray pron-toe)

It's not my decision.
No es mi decisión.
(No s-me day-sis-see-ohn.)

Keep checking in.
Vuélvate a hablarnos
(Bwell-bat-eh ah hab-lar-nose)

You're Hired!
Te Empleamos!
(Tay emp-lay-ah-mohs)

Paperwork
Papelería
(Pah-peh-lair-e-ah)

We need copies of ...
Necesitamos copias de ...
(Ness-cess-e-tahm-ohs coe-pee-ahs day ...)

Your Drivers License
Tu licencia de manejar
(Too lee-sen-see-ah day mahn-eh-har)

Social Security Card
Tarjeta de seguridad social
(Tar-het-ah day say-goo-ree-dahd so-see-ahl)

Green Card
La tarjeta verde
(La tar-hate-ah bair-day)

Birth Certificate
Certificado de nacimiento
(Sehr-tea-fee-kado day na-see-me-n-toe)

Passport
El pasaporte
(El pah-sah-port-eh)

Visa
Permiso de turista
(Pear-miso-day toor-e-stah)

Government
El gobierno
(El Go-bee-air-no)

Taxes
Los Impuestos
(Los eem-pweh-stows)

Deductions
Subtracciones
(Soob-trac-see-oh-nays)

Exemptions
Exenciones
(Ex-in-see-oh-nays)

Are you married? *
Estás casado?
(S-tahs ka-sa-thoe?)

Do you have children? *
Tienes niños?
(Tea-n-ehs knee-nyos?)

> *
> Though illegal to ask in most states, we provide these questions to assist in filling out I-9's and other tax related materials.

How Many? *
Cuántos tienes?
(Quan-tohs tea-n-ehs?)

The more exemptions you claim, the less taxes you will pay now.
De mas exenciones tu reclames, menos impuestos tu pagaras ahora.
(day mahs X-N-C-O-nays 2 reh-clah-mehs, meh-nohs eem-pweh-stohs 2 pah-gah-rahs ah-or-ah)

You might have to pay more taxes in April.
Tu podrias pagar mas impuestos en Abril.
(2 poh-dree-ahs pah-gahr mahs eem-pweh-stohs N ah-breel)

You might get some taxes back in April.
Tu podrias recibir impuestos de regreso en Abril.
(2 poh-dree-ahs reh-c-beer eem-pweh-stohs day reh-greh-soh N ah-breel)

I don't know enough about taxes to advise you.
Yo no se suficiente acerca de impuestos para aconsejarte.
(yo no say soo-fee-C-N-tay ah-sair-cah day eem-pweh-stohs pah-rah ah-cone-say-har-tay)

I am not allowed to advise you on taxes.
Yo no estoy permitido para aconsejarte sobre los impuestos.
(yo no S-toy pehr-me-t-doh pah-rah ah-cohn-say-har-tay soh-bray lohs eem-pweh-stohs)

Social Security
Seguro Social
(Say-goo-roh so-see-al)

Income Tax
Impuestos de ganancias
(Im-pwe-stows day gan-ahn-see-ahs)

Withholding
Retenido de antemano
(Ray-tin-e-doe day ahn-tea-man-oh)

Taxes are about (20) percent.
Quitan el (veinte) por ciento del cheque por los Impuestos.
(Key-tan el (bane-tay) poor see-en-toe del check-a poor los eem-pweh-stows.)

It is the law.
Es la ley
(S la lay)

Documentation
Documentación
(Doe-kooh-mehn-tah-see-ohn)

Laws / Legality
Leyes / Legalidad
(Lay-ehs) / (Lay-gal-e-dahd)

Illegal Alien
Un extranjero ilegal
(Oohn x-trahn-hair-o ill-e-gahl)

Immigration
La inmigración
(La in-me-gra-see-ohn)

Your pay is ($8) /hour.
Tu sueldo es (ocho dolares) a la hora.
(Too swell-doe s (o-cho doe-la-rays) ah la oar-ah)

Overtime pay is ...
Por horas extraordinarias es ...
(Poor oar-ahs x-tror-dee-nar-e-ahs s)

- **For over 40 hours / week.**
  Por más de cuarenta horas / A la semana.
  (Pour mahs day quar-n-tan oar-ahs / Ah-las say-mahn-ah)

- **For over 80 hours / two weeks.**
  Por más de ochenta horas / A las dos semanas.

  (Pour mahs day oh-chen-tah oar-ahs / Ah-las dose say-mahn-ahs)

- **For over 8 hours a day.**
  Por más de ocho horas / Al día.
  (Pour mahs day o-cho oar-ahs / Ahl dee-ah)

- **Time and a half.**
  El sueldo más la mitad
  (L swell-doe mahs la me-tahd)

- **Double Time**
  Tiempo doble
  (Tea-em-poe doe-blay)

- **Not permitted**
  No se permite
  (No say pear-me-tay)

When you have worked 40 hours, pack up and go home.
Cuando hayas trabajado cuarenta horas empaca y ve a casa.
(kwan-tho I-yahs trah-bah-ha-tho kwar-n-tah or-ahs, m-pah-cah E beh ah cah-sah)

You get paid on ____(Friday)______
Te pagamos los (Viernes)
(Tay pah-ga-mose los (b-air-nays)).

I will pay you at the end of the day.
Yo te pagare al final de cada dia.
(yoh tay pah-gahr-ay ahl fee-nahl day ca-tha dee-ah)

I will pay you every Friday.
Yo te pagare cada viernes.
(yoh tay pah-gahr-ay cah-tha b-air-nays)

I will pay you when the job is finished.
Yo te pagare cuando el trabajo este terminando.
(yoh tay pah-gah-ray kwan-tho L tra-bah-ho s-tay tehr-mee-nah-tho)

It will take (3) weeks to get your first check.
Recibes el primer cheque en (tres) semanas.
(Ray-c-bays l pre-mare check-a en (trace) say-mahn-ahs)

Then every two weeks after that.
Los siguientes vienen cada quincena
(Los see-gwee-n-tays b-n-n cahtha kween-say-nah)

The pay period lasts two weeks.
El período de pagos es por quincena
(L pehr-e-oh-doe day pah-goes s poor kween-sehn-ah)

Can you make it until then?
Estás bien hasta entonces
(S-tahs bee-n ahs-tah en-tone ses)

Advances are not permitted.
No se permite adelantos / avances.
(*No say pear-me-tay ah-day-lan-toes / ah-bahn-sais)*

We will advance you no more than (200) dollars.
No se adelanta / avanza más de (doscientos) dólares.
(No say ah-day-lan-tah / ah-bahn-sa mahs day(dose c-n-toes) doe-lar-ehs).

Overtime
Tiempo extra
(Tea-m-poe ex-trah)

Vacation
Vacaciones
(Bah-kah-see-ohn-ehs)

Pay Day
Día de pago
(D-ah day pah-go)

Shift
Turno
(Toor-no)

Sick Pay
El pago por días de enfermedad
(L pah-go poor dee-ahs day n-fair-may-dahd)

Sick Days
Días de enfermedad
(Dee-ahs day n-fair-may-dahd)

Holiday Pay
El pago por los días de fiesta
(L pah-go poor los d-ahs day fee-s-tah)

Bonuses
Dinero extra / bono
(Dee-nare-oh ex-trah / boh-noh))

Raises
Aumento de salario
(Ow-men-toe day sahl-ar-e-oh)

You start on (Monday).
Empiezas el (lunes).
(M-pee-ay-sahs el (loo-nehs)

You get a raise in (6) weeks / (3) months.
Te dan un aumento en (seis) semanas / (tres) meses.
(Tay dahn oon ow-men-toe en (sace) say-mahn-ahs / (trace) may-ses)

You must cover your own shifts.
Tienes que cubrir tus turnos si no puedes trabajar.
(T-n-ehs k coo-breer toos toor-nos see no pway-days trah-bah-har).

Schedule requests must be made (5) days before the new schedule.
Pedidos del horario deben estar hecho (cinco) días antes del nuevo.
(Pay-thee-thohs del oh-rar-e-oh day-ben s-tar ay-cho (seen-coh) dee-ahs ahn-tays del nway-bo).

The new schedule hangs on (Thursdays).
El nuevo horario sera colocado cada Jueves.
(L nway-boh o-rah-re-oh she-rah co-lo-cah-tho cah-tha whay-behs)

Your schedule will be the same every week.
Tu horario sera el mismo cada semana.
(2 or-R-E-O sarah L mees-moh cah-dah seh-mah-nah)

Your schedule will change every week.
Tu horario cambiara cada semana.
(2 or-R-E-O cahm-B-R-ah cah-dah seh-mahn-ah)

The hours we work will change on daylight savings.
Las horas que trabajamos cambian cuando el horario del pais cambiar.
(lahs or-ahs K trah-bah-ha-mohs cahm-b-ahn kwan-doh L or-R-E-O dehl pice cahm-B-R)

Call ahead if you will be late.
Hay que llamar si vas a llegar tarde.
(I k yam-mar see bahs ah yeah-gar tar-deh)

Here is the company phone list.
Aqui esta la lista de telefono de la compañia.
(ah-key s-tah la lee-stah day teh-leh-fo-no day la cohm-pahn-E-yah)

Call this number.
Llama a este numero.
(yah-mah ah s-tay noo-mare-oh)

Do not come to work if you are sick.
No vengas si estás enfermo.
(No bayn-gahs see s-tahs n-fare-moe)

You must be on time.
Debes llegar a tiempo.
(Deh-behs yeah-gar ah tea-m-poe)

Meet here every day at (7:00).
Te encuentro aqui todos los dias a las siete (7).
(tay N-kwen-troh ah-key toh-thos los d-ahs ah las (C-et-eh))

You must wear a hard hat.
Tu tienes que usar casco.
(too T-N-ehs K ooh-sahr cahs-coh)

You must wear (steel toe) boots.
Tu tienes que usar botas (con puntas de hierro/fierro.)
(too T-N-ehs K ooh-sahr boh-tahs (cone poon-tahs day e-air-oh / fee-air-oh))

You must provide your own gloves.
Tu tienes que traer tus propios guantes.
(2 T-N-S K trah-air toose proh-P-ohs gwahn-tays)

I will provide water/gatorade/sodas.
Yo proveeré aqua/gatorade/refrescos.
(yoh proh-b-ray ahg-wha / gatorade / reh-freh-skohs)

I will provide lunch each day.
Yo comprare almuerzo cada dia.
(yoh cohm-prah-ray ahl-mwer-soh cah-tha d-ah)

You must provide you own lunch.
Tu tienes que traer tu propio almuerzo.
(too-T-N-ehs K trah-ear too pro-p-oh ahl-mwer-soh)

Don't use the phone.
No uses el teléfono
(No oou-ses el tay-lay-fo-no)

Only in an emergency.
Sólo en caso de emergencia
(So-low en cah-so day em-er-hen-see-ah)

Use the phone in the office.
Usa el teléfono en la oficina
(Ooh-sa el tay-lay-fo-no en la off-eh-see-nah)

Use the pay phone.
Usa el teléfono público.
(Ooh-sa el tay-lay-fo-no poo-bleak-oh)

You get (30) minutes break per shift.
Se recibe (treinta) minutos por descanso.
(See ray-see-bay (tray-n-tah) mean-ooh-toes poor des-cahn so)

See a manager before you go on break.
Habla con el gerente antes de tomar descanso.
(Ahb-lah cone el hair-n-tay ahn-tays day toe-mar des-cahn-so)

No smoking inside.
Se prohibe fumar adentro.
(Say pro-he-bay foo-mar ah-den-troh)

Here's the time clock.
Esta es El reloj registrador
(S-tah S L ray-loh reh-he-stra-door)

Punch In / Out
Punchar la llegada / La Salida
(Poon-char la yeah-gahd-ah / La Sah-lee-tha)

Let's get started
Vamos a empezar.
(Bah-mose a em-peh-sar)

Notes
Apuntes
(Ah-poon-tehs)

How do you say _______________ in Spanish ?
Cómo se dice _______________ en Español?
(Koe-moe say d-say __________ en s-pahn-yohl?)

Notes
Apuntes
(Ah-poon-tehs)

How do you say ______________ in Spanish ?
Cómo se dice ______________ en Español?
(Koe-moe say d-say _________ en s-pahn-yohl?)

Don't Hurt Yourself.

Phrases to help you avoid using the material in Chapter 7

If you don't understand, ask for help.
Si no comprendes, pide ayuda.
(see no cohm-pren-dehs, p-day I-you-dah)

Carry knives point down, blade to the back.
Lleva los cuchillos con la punta hacia abajo y con la hoja hacia atrás.
(Yeah-bah los coo-che-yohs cone la poon-tah ah-c-ah ah-bah-ho e cone la o-ha ah-c-ah ah-trahs)

Don't use dull tools.
No uses herramientas desafiladas.
(No u-sehs air-rah-me-n-tahs dehs-ah-fee-lah-dahs)

Don't use damaged tools.
No use herramientas dañadas.
(no ooh-seh air-rah-me-n-tahs dah-nyah-thas)

Put the tools away when you are done.
Cuando termines con las herramientas guárdalas.
(Kwan-doe tehr-me-nehs cone lahs ai-rah-me-n-tahs gwar-dah-lahs).

Don't leave the handles sticking out.
No dejes que las asas sobresalgan.
(No day-hays k las ah-sahs so-bray-sahl-gahn)

Do not talk while you are using this.
No hables mientras usar esto.
(No ah-blays me-n-trahs ooh-sahr s-toe)

Make sure all parts are secure before you turn it on.
Asegura que todas las partes estén seguras antes de encenderlo.
(Ah-say-goo-rah k toe-das las par-tays s-ten seh-goo-rahs ahn-tays day n-sehn-dare-low)

Don't wear jewelry while you are using this.
Quítate las joyas antes de usar esto.
(Key-tah-tay las hoyas ahn-tays day ooh-sar s-toe)

Tuck in your shirt so it doesn't get caught.
Métete la camisa para que no se enganche.
(Meh-tet-eh la cah-me-sah pah-rah k no say n-gahn-chay)

Don't take your eyes off of it.
No pares de mirarlo.
(No par-ays day me-rar-low)

Use the feed arm (handle)
Usa la manija.
(Ooh-sah la mahn-e-ha)

Make sure the breaker is turned off first.
Asegurate que la electricidad este apagada.
(ah-seh-goo-rah-tay K la l-ek-triss-e-dahd s-tay ah-pah-gah-tha)

Unplug it before you touch it / clean it.
Desconéctalo antes de tocarlo / de limpiarlo.
(Dehs-cone-eck-tah-low ahn-tehs day toe-car-low / day lim-p-r-low).

Don't touch this until it stops completely.
No toques esto hasta que pare completamente.
(No toe-kays s-toe ah-stah k pah-ray come-pleh-tah-men-tay)

If you have to walk away, be sure to turn it off first.
Si tienes que irte apágalo primero.
(C t-n-ays k ear-tay ah-pah-gah-low pre-mare-oh)

Unplug it and cover it when you are done.
Desenchúfalo y cúbrelo cuando has terminado.
(Dehs-n-choo-fa-low e coo-bray-low kwan-doe ahs ter-me-nah-doe).

Don't touch this if your hands are wet.
No toques esto si las manos están mojadas.
(No toe-kways s-toe c las mahn-ohs s-tahn moe-ha-das)

Don't stand on wet ground while using this.
No te pares en tierra mojada cuando uses esto.
(no tay pah-rehs N T-air-ah moe-ha-tha kwan-doh ooh-sehs S-toh)

These chemicals are very strong. Don't get any on your skin.
Estos químicos son muy fuertes. Evita el contacto con la piel.
(S-toes key-me-cos sone moo-e fwer-tays. Eh-b-tah l cone-tact-oh cone la p-l)

Use rubber gloves when working with this stuff.
Usa los guantes de goma cuando trabajes con estas cosas.
(ooh-sah lohs gwan-tays day goh-mah kwan-tho tra-bah-hays cone s-tahs coh-sahs)

Wear safety glasses when doing this. Usas tus lentes de seguridad cuando estes haciendo esto aquello.
(ooh-sahs toose lehn-tehs day seh-goo-re-dahd kwan-tho s-tays ah-c-n-tho s-toe ah-kway-yoh)

Use a back brace while working with this material.
Usa el suspensor para la espalda mientras trabajes con este material.
(ooh-sah L suh-spehn-sohr pah-rah la s-pahl-dah me-n-trahs trah-bah-hehs cone s-tay mah-teer-e-ahl)

I will show you how to wear a safety harness.
Yo te mostrare como ponerte el cinturon de seguridad.
(yoh tay moh-strahr-eh coh-moh pohn-air-tay L seen-too-rohn day seh-goo re-dahd)

This MUST be locked.
Esto tiene que estar cerrado.
(s-toh T-N-A K S-tahr sehr-rah-tho)

Check it twice.
Verificalo dos veces.
(beh-riff-e-cah-loh dohs beh-sehs)

Always use a broom to pick up broken glass.
Siempre usa la escoba para recojer el vidrio roto.
(C-m-pray ooh-sah la s-co-bah pah-rah re-co-hair l bid-re-oh roe-toe)

Wipe up any spills immediately.
Si derramas algo límpialo inmediatamente.
(C dare-ah-mas ahl-go lim-p-ah-low in-me-d-ah-tah-men-tay)

Keep your face away when you open this.
Mantén alejada la cara cuando abres esto.
(Mahn-ten ahl-a-ha dah la cara kwan-doe ah-brays s-toe)

Make sure it is off before you walk away.
Asegura de que esté apagado antes de irte.
(Ah-say-goo-rah day K s-tay ah-pah-gah-tho ahn-tays day ear-tay)

Never assume the pilot light works.
Nunca asumas que la llama piloto está funcionando.
(Noon-cah ah-soo-mas k la yah-mah p-low-toe s-tah fun-c-o-non-doe)

Don't stack these too high.
No pongas estos en una pila muy alta.
(No pone-gahs s-toes n ooh-na p-lah moo-e ahl-tah)

Heavy things on the bottom, lighter things on top.
Pon las cosas pesadas debajo y las cosas ligeras encima.
(Pone las co-sahs pay-sah-dahs day bah-hoe e las co-sahs lee-hair-ahs n-c-mah)

Use the dolly/wheelbarrow.
Usa la carretilla/carreta.
(ooh-sah la carr-reh-t-yah / carr-reh-tah)

Lift with your legs.
Levanta con las piernas.
(Lay-bahn-tah cone las p-air-nahs)

Use both hands.
Usa las dos manos.
(Ooh-sah las dose mah-nose)

Always ask for help.
Siempre pide ayuda.
(C-m-pray p-day ah-you-dah)

Don't swing towards your feet.
No cortes / lanzes hacia tus pies.
(no cohr-tehs / lahn-sehs ah-c-ah toose p-a's)

Make sure no one is behind you.
Asegurate que nadie este detras de ti.
(ah-seh-goo-rah-tay K nah-thay s-tay deh-trahs day T)

Don't try to catch it if it falls, move away from it.
Si cae no trates de agarrarlo, muévete.
(C kah-ay no tra-tays day ah-gar-r-low mway-bet-a)

Cover it before you move it.
Cúbrelo antes de moverlo.
(Coo-bray-low ahn-tays day mow-bare-low)

Announce yourself when going around corners.
Si vienes detrás de alguien o vienes por la esquina siempre di algo <anúnciate>.
(See b-n-ace day-tras day ahl-gwee-n o b-n-ace pour la s-key-na, see-m-pray dee ahl-go. <ah-noon-c-ah-tay>)

Keep your work area clean and uncluttered.
Mantén tu área trabajadora limpia y organizada.
(Mahn-ten too ah-re-ah tra-bah-ha-door-ah lim-p-ah e or-gahn-e-sahd-ah)

Never run!!
Nunca corras.
(Noon-cah core-ahs)

Be careful.
Ten Cuidado.
(Tehn kwee-dahd-oh)

Pay attention.
Presta atención.
(Press-tah ah-ten-c-ohn)

Don't rush it.
No te apures.
(no tay ah-poo-rehs)

Calm down.
Calmate.
(cahl-mah-tay)

Get out of the sun for a few minutes.
Sal te del sol por unos pocos minutos.
(sahl tay dehl sohl poor ooh-nohs poh-cohs mee-noo-tohs)

Drink some water.
Toma agua.
(toe-mah agh-wah)

Use your eyes and ears at all times.
Usa los ojos y oidos todo el tiempo.
(ooh-sah lohs o-hohs E o-the-ohs toh-doh L T-M-poh)

Make sure you have 10 fingers and 10 toes when you are done.
Asegurate de tener diez dedos en tus manos y pies cuando hayas terminado.
(ah-seh-goo-rah-tay day teh-nehr D-S deh-dohs N toose mah-nohs E P-S kwan-tho I-yahs tehr-me-nah-tho)

Notes

Apuntes

(Ah-poon-tehs)

How do you say _______________ in Spanish ?

Cómo se dice _______________ en Español?

(Koe-moe say d-say __________ en s-pahn-yohl?)

Don't hurt my babies.

General instructions for operating and maintaining equipment.

This is where you put the key.
Aqui es donde tu pones las llaves.
(ah-key S dohn-day to poh-nehs las yah-behs)

This is how you turn it on.
Asi es como tu lo enciendes.
(ah-see S coh-moh to loh n-c-n-dehs)

The choke must be engaged to start it.
El ahogador debe estar en posición para empezarlo
(L ah-o-gah-door deh-beh s-tar N po-zih-c-ohn pah-rah m-peh-sahr-loh)

Check the fuel level every time you use it.
Chequea el nivel de la gasolina cada vez que lo uses.
(cheh-k-ah L nee-behl day la gahs-o-leena ca-tha behs K low ooh-sehs)

Oil and gas must be pre-mixed.
El aceite y la gasolina deben ser mezclados anteriormente.
(L ah-say-tay E la gahs-o-leena deh-behn sehr mehs-clah-tho ahn-teer-e-or-men-tay)

It takes unleaded fuel only.
Esto/eso solo usa gasolina sin plomo.
(s-toe / S-O solo usah gahs-o-leenah seen ploh-moh)

Check the air in the tires.
Revisa el aire en las ruedas/llantas/gomas.
(reh-beesah L I-ray N las yahn-tahs)

You must have the brake on before you can start it.
Tu debes tener pisado el freno antes de empezar.
(to deh-behs the-nair p-sah-thoe L freh-noh ahn-tays day m-peh-sahr)

Please show him/her how to operate it properly.
Por favor ensenale como operar/usar esto apropiadamente.
(poor fah-bore n-sin-ah-lay como oh-pear-r / ooh-sahr S-toh ah-pro-p-ah-tha-mehn-tay)

Can you drive a standard transmission?
Tu puedes manejar carros de transmision manual?
(to pweh-thes mahn-a-har car-rrohs day trahns-mis-e-ohn mah-nu-ahl)

Here is the parking brake.
Aqui esta el freno para estacionar.
(ah-key s-tah L fray-noh pah-rah s-tah-c-oh-nair)

The seat belt must be fastened to start it.
El cinturon de seguridad tiene que ser usado antes de prenderlo.
(L sin-to-rohn day she-goo-re-dahd t-n-a K sehr ooh-sa-tho ahn-tehs day prehn-dare-loh)

Please warm it up for (5) minutes before you start it.
Por favor calientalo por (cinco) minutos antes de usarlo/operarlo
(poor fah-bore cah-lee-in-tah-loh por (seen-coh) meh-noo-tohs ahn-tehs day ooh-sar-loh / o-pear-r-loh.)

Here is the throttle.
Aqui esta el acelarador.
(ah-key S-tah L ah-cell-r-ah-door)

Check the oil before each use.
Chequea el aceite antes de usarlo
(cheh-k-ah L ah-say-tay ahn-tays day ooh-sahr-lo).

Make sure it's on level ground before operating.
Asegurate que este al nivel de piso antes de usarlo.
(ah-seh-goo-rah-tay K S-tay ahl nee-behl day p-soh ahn-tays day ooh-sahr-lo)

Use safety glasses at all times.
Usa los lentes de seguridad todo el tiempo.
(ooh-sah los lehn-tays day seh-goo-re-dahd toe-tho L t-m-poe)

Use a hard hat at all times.
Usa el casco todo el tiempo.
(ooh-sah L cahs-co to-tho L t-m-poe)

This makes it go forward.
Esto lo hace ir hacia adelante.
(s-toh low ah-say ear ah-c-ah ah-dehl-ahn-tay)

This makes it go backwards.
Esto lo hace ir hacia atras.
(s-toh lo ah-say ear ah-c-ah ah-trahs)

This will engage the blades.
Esto conectara las hojillas.
(s-toh co-neck-tar-ah las hoe-E-yahs)

This is the emergency shut-off.
Este es el trancador de emergencia.
(s-tay S L trahn-cah-dohr day eh-mehr-hen-c-ah)

This is the kill switch.
Este es el boton para apagarlo
(s-tay S L boh-tohn pah-rah ah-pah-gahr-loh)

Here is the seat adjustment.
Este es el ajustador de la silla.
(s-tay S L ah-hoose-tah-dohr day la see-yah)

Have you operated this machine before.
Has usado esta maquina antes?
(ahs ooh-sah-tho s-tah mah-key-nah ahn-tays)

This will raise/lower the bucket.
Esto subira/bajara el pote.
(s-toh soo-bree-ah / bah-ha-rah L poh-tay)

This will rotate the bucket.
Esto girara/rotara el pote.
(s-toh hih-rah-rah / roh-tar-ah L poh-tay)

Keep your hands and arms clear of moving parts.
Manten las manos y las brazos alejados de las partes en movimiento.
(mahn-tehn lahs mah-nohs E lahs brah-sohs ah-lay-ha-thos day las par-tehs N moh-V-me-N-toh)

This will engage the drive.
Esto conectara el manejador.
(s-toh co-neck-tar-ah L mah-nay-ha-door)

Watch for overhead power lines.
Cuidado con las lineas de electricidad.
(kwee-dahd-oh cone lahs lee-nee-ahs day eh-lekt-riss-e-dahd.)

Are you comfortable with this equipment?
Te sientes confortable con este equipo?
(tay C-N-tays cohn-for-tah-blay cone S-tay eh-kwee-poh)

Show me how to use it.
Enseñame como usarlo.
(N-sin-yah-may coh-moh ooh-sahr-loh)

Trade off every (2 / 30) hours/minutes.
Cambia cada (dose / treinta) horas / minutos.
(cahm-b-ah cah-tha (doh-say / tray-n-tah) or-ahs / mee-noo-tohs)

Let me show you how.
Dejame enseñarte como.
(deh-ha-may N-sin-yar-tay coh-moh)

Watch out for stumps and rocks.
Cuidado con los tocónes y las piedras.
(kwee-dah-doh cone lohs toh-coh-nays E lahs p-eh-drahs)

----MAINTENANCE----

Change the oil after (100) hours of operation.
Cambia el aciete despues de (cien) horas de operacion.
(cahm-b-ah L ah-say-tay dehs-puehs day (C-N) or-ahs day oh-pear-ah-c-ohn)

Always check the belts before using.
Siempre revisa las correas antes de usarlo.
(C-M-pray reh-b-sah lahs corr-a-ahs ahn-tays day ooh-sahr-loh)

The blades must be sharpened every (7) days.
Las hojillas tienen que ser afiladas cada (siete) dias.
(las oh-he-yahs T-N-N K sehr ah-fee-lah-thas cah-tha (c-et-a) dee-ahs)

Clean the air filter before use.
Limpia el filtro de aire antes de usarlo.
(leem-p-ah L feel-troh day I-reh ahn-tays day ooh-sahr-loh)

Check the oil level.
Revisa el nivel del aceite.
(reh-b-sah L neh-behl del ah-say-tay)

Check the tire pressure.
Revisa la presion del aire.
(reh-b-sah la preh-c-ohn del I-reh)

Wash the machine after use.
Lava la maquina despues de usarla.
(lah-bah la mah-key-nah dehs-puehs day ooh-sahr-lah)

These are the lubrication points.
Estos son los puntos de lubricacion.
(s-tohs sone los poon-tohs day loo-breh-cah-c-ohn)

Use this lubricant only.
Usa esta lubricante solamente.
(ooh-sah s-tah loo-bree-cahn-tay sohl-ah-men-tay)

Grease the machine daily.
Engrasa la maquina todos los dias.
(n-grah-sah la mah-key-nah toh-doh los d-ahs)

Mix (8) gallons of gas and oil daily.
Mezcla (ocho) galones de gasolina y aceite diaramiente.
(mes-clah O-cho gah-loh-nays day gahs-o-lee-nah E ah-say-tay D-ah-rah-me-in-tay)

Fill the machines with gas daily.
Llena todas las maquinas con gasolina todos los dias.
(yeah-nah toh-dahs las mah-key-nahs cone gahs-oh-lina toh-dohs los d-ahs)

Inspect all moving parts daily.
Inspecciona todas las partes que se mueven diariamente.
(een-spec-c-ohn-ah toh-dahs las parh-tays K say mway-behn d-ah-rah-mehn-tay)

Report any strange noises coming from the equipment.
Reporta cualquier ruido extraño del equipo.
(reh-poor-tah kwal-key-air roo-E-tho x-trahn-yoh dehl eh-kwee-poh)

If the machine needs repair, take it to the shop.
Si la maquina necesita reparacion llevala al garage.
(see la mah-key-nah neh-ceh-c-tah reh-pahr-ah-c-ohn, yay-ball-ah ahl gah-rah-hay)

Ask for help when lifting heavy objects.
Pregunta por ayuda cuando vayas a levantar objetos pesados.
(preh-goon-tah poor I-U-dah kwan-doh buy-ahs ah leh-bahn-tahr ohb-hect-ohs peh-sah-thos)

Use a jack stand when working under equipment.
Usa el levantador cuando trabajes debajo de este equipo.
(ooh-sah L leh-bahn-tah-dohr kwan-doh trah-bah-hays deh-bah-hoh dya s-tay eh-keep-oh)

Thank you for being careful with it.
Gracias por ser cuidadoso con esto.
(grah-c-ahs poor sehr kwee-dah-doh-soh cone S-toh)

Don't park near red signs.
No estaciones cerca señales rojas.
(noh s-tah-c-o-nays sehr-cah sehn-yahl-ehs row-haas)

Don't park next to fire hydrants.
No estaciones cerca de los hidrantes de agua.
(no s-tah-c-o-nays sehr-cah day lohs e-drahn-tays day ah-gwah)

Give the parking tickets to me immediately.
Dame los tickets de trafico a me inmediatamente.
(dah-may lohs t-kets day trah-fee-coh ah me een-me-d-ah-tah-men-tay)

Notes

Apuntes

(Ah-poon-tehs)

How do you say _______________ in Spanish ?

Cómo se dice _______________ en Español?

(Koe-moe say d-say __________ en s-pahn-yohl?)

Notes
Apuntes
(*Ah-poon-tehs*)

How do you say _______________ in Spanish ?
Cómo se dice _______________ en Español?
(Koe-moe say d-say __________ en s-pahn-yohl?)

Lets get it done!

Phrases for every step of installation.

- Demolition and preparation
- Sprinklers and irrigation
- Sod and bedding
- Planting
- Light Masonry
- Clean up

DEMOLITION AND PREPARATION

We will begin here.
Nosotros comenzaremos aqui.
(noh-soh-trohs coh-mehn-sah-ray-mohs ah-key)

We will finish here.
Nosotros terminaremos/finalizaremos aqui.
(*noh-soh-trohs tehr-me-nahr-a-mohs / fih-nahl-e-sahr-a-mohs ah-key)*

Remove everything in this area.
Remueve todo en esta area.
(reh-mweh-beh toe-doh N s-tah ah-re-ah)

Always wear safety glasses.
Usa siempre los lentes de seguridad.
(ooh-sah c-m-pray los lehn-tays day seh-goo-re-dahd)

Use a (pick axe) for best results.
Usa la (pica) para mejor resultado.
(ooh-sah lah (p-cah) pah-rah may-whore reh-sool-tah-thoe)

Do not drive over this area with the tractor.
No manejes el tractor en esta area.
(no mah-nay-hays L tractor N s-tah r-e-ah)

Put down a wood path through here.
Coloca un camino de madera atraves de aqui.
(coh-loh-cah oohn cah-me-noh day mah-dare-ah ah-trah-behs day ah-key)

Do not drive over this area with a wheelbarrow.
No manejas la carreta en esta area.
(no mah-nay-hass la car-ret-ah N s-tah r-e-ah)

Follow this line.
Sigue la linea.
(c-gway la lin-e-ah)

Remove all the rocks and debris.
Remueve todas las rocas y escombros.
(reh-mweh-bay toe-dahs lahs roh-cahs E s-comb-rohs)

Dig up all the roots.
Remueve/quita todas las raices.
(reh-mweh-bay / kwee-tah toe-dahs las rye-sais)

Use a chain to remove this.
Usa la cadena para remover esto.
(ooh-sah la cah-day-nah pah-rah (reh-moh-behr s-toe)
Stand clear during removal.
Ten cuidado durante el removimiento.
(tehn-kwee-dah-doh doo-rahn-tay L reh-moh-b-me-N-toh)

Do not remove this tree/shrub.
No remuevas/quites este arbol.
(no reh-mweh-bahs / kwee-tehs s-tay ahr-bohl)

Be careful of sprinkler lines.
Ten quidado con las lineas de la regadera.
(tehn kwee-da-thoe cone las lee-nee-ahs day la reh-gah-dare-ah)

Be careful of power lines/wiring.
Ten cuidado con las lineas de electricidad.
(tehn kwee-dahd-oh cone las lih-nee-ahs day L-ek-triss-e-dahd)

There are utilities located here.
Aqui estan las lineas de electricidad.
(ah-key s-tahn lahs lee-nee-ahs day ehl-eck-triss-e-dahd)

Place markers/flags at each sprinkler head location.
Coloca las banderas en la cabeza de cada regadera.
(*coh-loh-cah las bahn-dehr-ahs N la cah-bay-sah day cah-tha reh-hah-dare-ah)*

Watch out for flags/markers.
Esta pendiente con las banderas.
(s-tah penh-d-n-tay cone las bahn-dare-ahs)

Use the tractor to remove the rocks.
Usa el tractor para remover las rocas.
(ooh-sah ehl tractor pah-rah reh-moh-behr las row-cahs)

Empty all waste into the dumpster.
Pon/coloca toda la basura en el basurero.
(pone / coh-loh-cah toe-dah la bah-soo-rah N L bah-soo-rare-oh)

Empty all waste into the truck/trailer.
Pon/coloca toda la basura dentro de la truca/camion.
(pone / coh-loh-cah toe-dah la bah-soo-rah dehn-troh day la troo-cah / cah-me-ohn)

The dumpster is not for our use.
El basurero no es para nuestro uso.
(L bah-soo-rare-oh no s pah-rah noo-a-stroh ooh-soh)

Cover your load before transporting.
Cubre el cargamento antes de transportarlo.
(coo-bray L car-gah-men-toh ahn-tehs day trahns-port-r-loh)

Use water to keep the dust down.
Use el agua para mantener el polvo abajo.
(ooh-say L ahg-wah pah-rah mahn-tehn-air L pohl-boh ah-bah-hoe)

Use a tarp to protect this area.
Usa el cobertor para protejer esta area.
(ooh-sah L co-bare-tohr pah-rah pro-teh-hair s-tah r-e-ah)

Get help to lift heavy objects.
Busca ayuda para leventar los objetos pesados.
(boo-skah I-you-tha pah-rah leh-behn-tahr los ohb-hect-ohs pehs-ah-thohs)

This area needs to be level.
Esta area necesita ser nivelada.
(s-tah r-e-ah neh-ceh-c-tah sehr nee-behl-ah-tha)

Grade this area smooth.
Nivela esta area.
(nee-behl-ah S-tah ah-re-ah)

Use weed barrier along here.
Usa el rastrillo por aqui.
(ooh-sah L rahs-tree-yoh poor ah-key)

Follow this line for steel edging.
Sique esta linea para el fierro.
(see-gway s-tah lih-nee-ah pah-rah L fee-air-oh)

Use plenty of pins/stakes to secure this.
Usa suficientes clavos para asegurar esto.
(*ooh-sah soo-fiss-e-n-tehs clah-bohs pah-rah ah-say-goo-rahr s-toe)*

This area should be higher / lower.
Esta area deberia ser mas alta / baja.
(s-tah r-e-ah deh-bare-ah sehr mahs ahl-tah / bah-ha)

Move it to the right/left.
Muevelo a la derecha / izquierda.
(mway-bay-loh ah la deh-reh-cha / iss-kwee-air-dah)

Move it further back/forward.
Muevlo hacia atras/adelante.
(mway-bay-loh ah-c-ah ah-trahs / ah-dehl-ahn-tay)

Remove a little more.
Remueve en poquito mas.
(reh-mweh-beh N poe-key-toe mahs)

Add a little more.
Añade un poco mas.
(ahn-yah-day oohn poe-coe mahs)

Get some help to move that.
Busca ayuda para mover eso.
(boo-skah I-U-dah pah-rah moh-behr S-O)

Be careful when backing up.
Ten cuidado cuando retrocedas.
(tehn-kwee-dah-doh kwan-doh reh-troh-ceh-dahs)

Have someone look out for you.
Ten a alguien mirando por ti.
(tehn ah ahl-ghee-in mee-rahn-doh poor T)

Cover this area before driving on it.
Cubre esta area antes de manejar sobre ella.
(coo-bray S-tah ah-re-ah ahn-tays day mahn-eh-har soh-bray A-yah)

Tie down your load before moving.
Atar bien tu cargamento antes de moverte.
(ah-tahr b-n 2 cahr-gah-men-toh ahn-tehs day moh-behr-tay)

Move all sprinkler heads to the edge.
Mueve todas las cabezas de agua hacia los bordes.
(mweh-bay toe-dahs lahs cah-bay-sahs day ah-gwah ah-c-ah lohs bohr-dehs)

Wet this area to keep the dust down.
Moja esta area para mantener el polvo en el piso.
(moe-ha s-tah ah-re-ah pah-rah mehn-tehn-air L pohl-boh N L p-soh)

This must be finished today.
Esto tiene que ser terminado hoy.
(s-toh T-N-A K sehr tehr-me-nah-doh oy)

This must be ready by (Tuesday).
Esto tiene que ser terminado para el Martes.
(s-toh T-N-A K sehr tehr-me-nah-doh pah-rah L mahr-tehs)

Use manure / compost here.
Usa el estiércol aqui.
(ooh-sah L s-t-air-coal ah-key)

Till the soil first.
Labra / Cultiva esta tierra primero.
(lah-brah / cool-t-bah s-tah t-air-ah pre-mare-oh)

Use the trimmer to clear the weeds.
Usa la cortadora para limpiar las hierbas malas.
(ooh-sah lah core-tah-door-ah pah-rah leem-p-ahr lahs e-air-bahs mah-lahs)

Use a mower to clear this area.
Usa la cortacésped para limpiar esta area.
(ooh-sah lah core-tah-seh-sped pah-rah leem-p-ahr s-tah ah-re-ah)

Use a chainsaw.
Usa el motosierra.
(ooh-sah L moh-toh-c-air-ah)

Put all debris in the chipper/shredder.
Pon todos los escombros en el trituradora.
(pone toh-dohs lohs s-cohm-brohs N L tree-2-rah-door-ah)

Use the shredded material for mulch.
Usa todo el material picado como pajote.
(ooh-sah toh-doh L mah-teh-re-ahl p-cah-doh coh-moh pah-hoe-tay)

Sprinklers and Irrigation

We will begin here.
Comenzaremos aqui
(co-men-sah-ray-mose ah-key)

This is the water source.
Esta es la fuente del agua.
(s-tah S la fwen-tay dehl ah-gwa)

The manifold goes here.
Este tubo/manguera va aqui.
(s-tay too-bow / mahn-gwer-ah bah ah-key)

The lines run in this direction.
Las lineas corren en esta direccion.
(las lin-e-ahs corr-rehn N s-tah d-rec-c-ohn)

We will trench from here to there.
Abriremos el hueco de aqui hasta alla.
(ahb-re-ray-mohs L hway-coe day ah-key ah-stah ah-yah)

Make the trench at least (6) in. / ft. deep.
Haz el hueco al menos (seis) pulgadas / pies.
(oz L hway-co ahl meh-nohs (sace) pool-gah-thas / p-ehs)

We will run (4) separate lines.
Pondremos (cuatro) diferentes lineas.
(pone-dreh-mohs (kwa-troh) dee-fehr-N-tehs lee-nee-ahs)

There are (3) zones.
Aqui hay (tres) zonas
(ah-key I (trace) soh-nahs)

There are (2) zones in the front.
Aqui hay (dos) zones en el frente.
(ah-key I (dose) sohn-ehs N L frehn-tay)

There are (7) zones in the rear.
Aqui hay (siete) zones en la parte trasera.
(ah-key I (c-et-a) sohn-ehs N la par-tay trah-sehr-ah)

There are (5) heads in this zone.
Aqui hay (cinco) cabezas en esta zona.
(ah-key I (seen-coh) cah-bay-sahs N s-tah soh-na)

Place one sprinkler head here.
Coloca una cabeza de la regadera aqui.
(co-loh-cah ooh-nah cah-bay-sah day la reh-ha-dare-ah ah-key)

Use a (90 degree) nozzle here.
Usa la boquilla (noventa grados) aqui.
(ooh-sah la boh-key-yah (noh-behn-tah grah-dohs) ah-key)

Install the clock here.
Instala el reloj aqui.
(N-stall-ah L reh-low ah-key)

Make sure this line is under the fabric.
Asegurate que esta linea este debajo del plastico.
(ah-she-goo-rah-tay K s-tah lihn-e-ah s-tay deh-bah-hoe dehl plah-stee-coe)

Use stakes to hold the line in place.
Usa las estacas para sostener la linea en su lugar.
(ooh-sah lahs s-tah-cahs pah-rah soh-sten-air la lihn-e-ah N soo loo-gahr)

Pull the tubing through the fabric before you cover it.
Jalar el tubo a traves del tela antes de cubrirlo.
(hah-lahr L too-boh ah trah behs del teh-lah ahn-tays day coo-breer-low)

Test all zones before burying.
Prueba todas las zonas antes de cubrirlo.
(proo-way-bah toe-dahs lahs soh-nahs ahn-tehs day coo-breer-loh))

Are there any leaks in the system.
Hay algun hueco / hoyos en el sistema.
(I ahl-goon hway-coh / oy-ohs N L sees-t-mah)

Use two clamps for each connection.
Usa dos ganchos para cada coneccion.
(ooh-sah dose gahn-chos pah-rah ca-dah co-neck-c-ohn)

Make these heads level with the ground.
Coloca estas cabezas al mismo nivel
(co-low-cah S-tahs cah-bay-sahs ahl mees-moh nih-behl).

Raise these heads (2) inches.
Sube estas cabezas (dos) pulgadas.
(soo-bay s-tahs cah-bay-sahs (dose) pool-gah-thas)

Follow the paint markings when trenching.
Sigue las marcas de la pintura cuando abra los huecos.
(see-gway las mahr-cahs day la peen-too-rah kwan-doh ah-brah lohs hway-cohs)

Trench this area first. Second. Third. Last.
Abre los huecos en esta area primero. Segundo. Tercero. Ultimo.
(ah-bray lohs hway-cohs N s-tah r-e-ah pre-mare-oh / she-goon-doh / tehr-sare-oh / ool-t-moh)

This is the electrical source.
Esta es la fuente de electicidad.
(s-tah S la fwen-tay day eh-lect-riss-e-dahd)

Use (3/4) in. tubing/ pipe.
Usa (tres cuartos) pulgadas tubo.
(ooh-sah (trace kwar-tohs) pool-gah-dahs too-boh)

We must finish today / tomorrow.
Tenemos que terminar hoy / manana.
(teh-neh-mose K tear-me-nahr oy / mahn-yahn-ah)

Call me if you need help.
Llamame si necesitas ayuda.
(yah-mah-may see neh-seh-see-tahs I-u-tha)

Start in the front/rear.
Empieza en el frente/ en la parte de atras.
(m-p-a-sah N L frehn-tay / N al par-tay day ah-trahs)

I will set the clock.
Yo colocare el reloj.
(yo coh-loh-car-eh L reh-loh)

This is how you set the clock.
Asi es como tu colocas el reloj.
(ah-see S coh-moh too coh-lo-cahs L reh-loh)

Run the electric lines from here to here.
Coloca las lineas de electricidad de aqui hasta aqui.
(coh-loh-cah las leen-e-ahs day ehl-ekt-riss-e-dahd day ah-kee ah-stah ah-key)

Use (4) wires.
Usa (cuatro) cables.
(ooh-sah (kwah-troh) cah-blehs)

Place the valve box here.
Coloca la caja de vavulas aqui.
(coh-loh-cah la ca-hah day bahl-boo-lahs ah-key)

Raise/lower the valve box.
Sabe/ baja la caja de valvulas.
(sah-bay / ba-ha la cah-ha day bahl-boo-lahs)

Make it level.
Hazlo a nivel.
(ahs-loh ah nee-behl)

Test the system again.
Pruebe el sistema otra vez.
(proo-eh-bay L see-stee-mah o-trah behs)

Use the clock to test the system.
Usa el reloj para probar el systema.
(ooh-sah L reh-loh pah-rah pro-bahr L sees-teem-ah)

Here is the problem.
Aqui esta el problema.
(ah-key s-tah L proh-blem-ah)

Do you have any problems?
Tienes algun problemas.
(t-n-s ahl-goon proh-blem-ahs)

Where is the problem?
Donde está el problema.
(dohn-day S-tah L proh-blem-ah)

Ask him /her for help.
Preguntale a el/ ella por ayuda.
(preh-goon-tah-lay ah L / a-yah poor ah-you-dah)

Ask him/her to demonstrate.
Preguntale a el / ella para demostrar.
(preh-goon-tah-lay ah L / a-yah pah-rah deh-mohn-strahr)

Show him/her how to do this.
Ensañale a el/ ella.
(n-sahn-yah-lay ah L / a-yah)

I will demonstrate.
Yo le demosraré.
(yoh lay deh-mo-strahr)

All the parts are in the truck.
Todas las partes estan en el troca.
(toe-dahs las par-tehs s-tahn N L troh-cah)

All the parts are in the box.
Todos las partes estan en la caja.
(toe-dohs lahs par-tehs s-tahn N L cah-hah)

Do you need any parts?
Necesitas algunas partes?
(neh-seh-c-tahs ahl-goon-ahs par-tehs)

Do you have all the tools?
Tienes todas las herramientas?
(t-n-s- toe-dahs lahs air-ah-me-n-tahs)

I will return with parts.
Yo regresare con los repuestos.
(yoh reh-greh-sahr-eh cone lohs reh-pweh-stohs)

SOD AND BEDDING

Follow the lines.
Sigue las lineas.
(see-gway lahs lee-nee-ahs)

Use steel edging here.
Usa el bordes de fierro aqui.
(ooh-sah L bohr-dehs day fee-air-roh ah-key)

Use safety cap on the edging.
Usa el tapón de seguridad en el fierro.
(ooh-sah L tah-pohn day seh-goo-re-dahd N L fee-air-oh)

Put fabric here.
Coloca la tela aqui.
(coh-loh-cah lah teh-lah ah-key)

Use the fabric before you plant.
Usa la tela antes de plantar.
(ooh-sah lah teh-lah ahn-tays day plahn-tahr)

Use fabric after you plant.
Usa la tela despues de plantar.
(ooh-sah lah teh-lah dehs-puehs day plahn-tahr)

Use flags to mark all sprinkler heads.
Usa banderas para marcar todas las cabezas de agua.
(ooh-sah bahn-deh-rahs pah-rah mar-cahr toe-dahs lahs cah-bay-sahs day ahg-wah)

Grade the entire area smooth before you start.
Gradua la area entera antes de empezar.
(grah-do-ah lah ah-re-ah n-tare-ah ahn-tays day eem-pay-sahr)

Remove all rocks and debris.
Remueve todas las rocas y escombros.
(reh-mweh-bay toe-dahs lahs roe-cahs E s-cohm-brohs)

Make the rock / gravel (6) in. deep.
Coloca las rocas / gravilla (seis) pulgadas de profundidad.
(coh-loh-cah lahs roh-cahs / grah-b-yah (sase) pool-gah-thas day pro-foon-d-dahd)

Use a wheelbarrow to move the rock/gravel.
Usa la carretilla para mover las rocas / gravilla.
(ooh-sah lah cahr-reht-t-yah pah-rah moh-behr lahs roh-cahs / grah-b-yah)

Use a scoop shovel.
Usa la pala.
(ooh-sah lah pah-lah)

Use a flat shovel.
Usa la pala plana.
(ooh-sah lah pah-lah plah-nah)

Use a rake.
Usa el rastrillo.
(ooh-sah L rahs-tree-yoh)

Don't use a rake.
No uses el rastrillo.
(no ooh-sehs L rahs-tree-yoh)

Make it deeper here.
Hazlo mas profundo aqui.
(ahs-loh mahs pro-foon-doh ah-key)

Make it shallower here.
No lo hagas profundo aqui.
(no loh ah-gahs pro-foon-doh ah-key)

Smooth this area.
Nivela esta area.
(nee-behl-ah s-tah ah-re-yah)

Cover this area completely.
Cubre esta area completamente.
(coo-bray s-tay ah-re-ah cohm-plet-ah-men-tay)

Set out all the sod before you unroll it.
Coloca afuera todo el celote antes de desenrrollarlo
(coh-loh-cah ah-fwer-ah toe-doh L ceh-loh-tay ahn-tays day dehs-n-rroh-yahr-loh)

Use wet burlap to prevent drying.
Usa el saco mojado para prevenir que se seque.
(ooh-sah L sah-coh mo-ha-tho pah-rah preh-beh-neer K say seh-gway)

Keep the sod in the shade.
Coloca el celote en la sombra.
(coh-loh-cah L ceh-loh-tay N la sohm-brah)

Unload the truck here.
Descarga la truca aqui.
(dehs-cahr-gah lah troo-cah ah-key)

We need (3) pallets.
Nosotros necesitamos (tres) pallets.
(noh-soh-trohs neh-seh-tah-mohs (trace) pah-let-ehs)

We need (20) rolls.
Nosotros necesitamos (veinte) rollos.
(no-soh-trohs neh-seh-c-tah-mohs (bain-tay) roh-yohs)

Lay out (40) rolls first.
Extiendas (cuarenta) rollos primero.
(x-t-n-dahs (kwar-n-tah) roh-yohs pre-mare-oh)

You lay out the rolls while he / she installs them.
Tu extiendas los rollos mientras el / ella los instala.
(too x-t-n-dahs lohs roh-yohs me-n-trahs L / a-yah lohs een-stahl-ah)

Green side up.
La parte verde hacia arriba.
(la par-tay behr-day ah-c-ah ahr-ree-bah)

Sharpen your knife.
Afila tu cuchillo.
(ah-fee-lah too coo-chee-yoh)

Watch how I do it.
Mira como lo hago.
(mee-rah coe-moh loh ah-goh)

Show him / her how to do it.
Enseñale a el / ella como hacerlo.
(een-sehn-yahl-a ah L / a-yah coe-moh ah-sehr-loh)

Please pay attention.
Por favor presta atencion.
(poor fah-bohr prehs-tah ah-ten-c-ohn)

Run the sod perpendicular to the building.
Coloca el celote perpendicularmente al edificio.
(coh-loh-cah L ceh-lo-tay pehr-pen-deek-ooh-lahr-men-tay ahl ehd-e-fee-c-oh)

Run the sod parallel to the building.
Coloca el celote paralelamente al edificio.
(coh-loh-cah L ceh-lo-tay pah-rah-lel-ah-men-tay ahl ehd-e-fee-c-oh)

Stagger the seams of each row.
Alterna las ranuras de cada linea.
(ahl-tehr-nah lahs rah-noo-rahs day cah-dah lee-nee-ah)

Don't leave any gaps.
No dejes ningun hueco o vacio.
(no deh-hehs neen-goon hway-coh O bah-c-oh)

Start at the edging.
Empieza en el borde.
(eem-p-a-sah ehn L bohr-day)

Start at the bottom of the hill.
Empieza en la parte de abajo de la colina.
(eem-p-a-sah N la par-tay day ah-bah-hoe lah coh-lee-nah)

Start at the top of the hill.
Empieza en la parte de arriba de la colina.
(eem-p-a-sah N lah par-tay day ahr-re-bay day la co-lee-nah)

Use a full roll here.
Usa un rollo completo aqui.
(ooh-sah oohn roh-yoh cohm-plet-oh ah-key)

Use the scrap pieces here.
Usa las pequeñas piezas aqui.
(ooh-sah lahs peh-kwane-yahs p-a-sahs ah-key)

Don't waste any pieces.
No desperdicies ninguna piezas.
(no dehs-pehr-d-c-ehs neen-goon-ah p-a-sahs)

Clean the edges thoroughly.
Limpia los bordes completamente.
(leem-p-ah lohs bohr-days cohm-pleht-ah-men-tay)

Edges should be (4) in. deep.
El borde debe ser (cuatro) pulgadas de profundidad.
(L bore-day deh-bay sehr (kwa-troh) pool-gah-thas day pro-foon-d-dahd)

The sod will settle.
El celote la grama asentara.
(L ceh-loh-tay lah grah-mah ah-seen-tah-rah)

Water thoroughly when finished.
Mojalo completamente cuando este terminado.
(mo-hall-oh cohm-plet-ah-mehn-tay kwan-tho s-tay tehr-me-nan-doh)

Use the drum roller when you are finished.
Usa el rodillo cuando tu hayas terminado.
(ooh-sah L roh-d-yoh kwan-doh 2 I-yahs tehr-me-nah-doh)

Finish this area before lunch.
Termina esta area antes de almorzar.
(tehr-mee-nah s-tah ah-re-ah ahn-tays day ahl-mohr-sahr)

Finish this area before dark.
Termina esta area antes de oscurezca.
(tehr-mee-nah s-tah ah-re-ah ahn-tays oh-skoo-reh-ska)

Don't walk on the sod when it's wet.
No camines en el celote cuando este mojado.

(no cah-me-nays N L ceh-loh-tay kwan-doh s-tay mo-ha-tho)
Save all the scrap pieces.
Guarda todo lo que sobre de celote.
(gwar-dah toe-doh loh K soh-bray day ceh-loh-tay)

Throw away the scrap pieces.
Bota todas las piezas que sobran.
(boh-tay toe-dahs lahs p-a-sahs K soh-brahn)

These edges need to be closer / tighter.
Esos bordes necesitan ser cerrados apretadamente.
(s-ohs bohr-dehs neh-seh-c-tahn sehr cehr-rah-thohs ah-preh-tah-dah-men-tay)

PLANTING

Start with the trees.
Comienza con los arboles.
(co-me-n-sah cone lohs ahr-bow-lehs)

Shrubs are planted second.
Los arbustos de segundo.
(lohs ahr-boo-stohs day seh-goon-doh)

We will start here.
Comenzaremos aqui.
(co-men-sah-ray-mohs ah-key)

We will end here.
Terminaremos aqui.
(tear-meen-ah-ray-mohs ah-key)

Make the hole (2) ft. deep and (3) ft. wide.
Haz el hoyo (dos) pies profundo y (tres) pies ancho.
(ahs el oy-yo (dohs) p-ehs pro-foon-doh E (trace) p-ehs ahn-cho.)

Dig that hole a little deeper.
Escava ese hoyo mas profundo.
(s-cah-bah s-a oy-yo mahs pro-food-d-doh)

That hole is too deep.
Ese hoyo es muy profundo.
(s-a oy-yo s moo-e pro-foon-d-doh)

Back-fill with soil and fertilizer.
Rellenalo con tierra y fertilizante
(ray-ehn-ah loh cone t-air-ah E fehr-til-ih-sahn-tay)

Face the nicest side out.
Pon la parte mas bonita hacia afuera.
(pone la par-tay mahs bow-knee-tah ah-see-ah ah-fwer-ah)

Beware of utility lines.
Cuidado con las lineas de electricidad.
(kwee-dahd-oh cone las lihn-e-ahs day eh-lekt-riss-e-dahd)

Beware of sprinkler lines.
Cuidado con las lineas de riego.
(kwee-dahd-oh cone las lihn-e-ahs day ree-eh-hoe)

Create a dam for water retention.
Crea un dique para retener agua.
(cree-ah oohn d-kway pah-rah reh-tehn-air ah-gwa)

Water in all plants after planting.
Riega las plantas después de la plantarlas.
(ree-ha las plahn-tahs dehs-pwehs day la plahn-tar-lahs)

Use fertilizer before/after planting.
Usa el fertilizante antes/después de plantar.
(ooh-sah L fer-tih-lih-sahn-tay ahn-tehs / dehs-puehs day plahn-tahr)

Keep the ball covered with wet burlap.
Manten la pelota cubierta con el saco mojado.
(mahn-tehn la peh-low-tah coo-b-air-tah cone L sah-coh moe-ha thoe)

Use the ball cart to move that.
Usa la carretilla de bola para mover eso.
(ooh-sah la cah-reh-t-yah day boh-lah pah-rah mow-behr S-O)

Do not unwrap the ball before it's in the hole.
No remuevas el saco de la pelota antes de que este en el hoyo.
(no reh-mway-bahs L sah-coh day la pay-low-tah ahn-tehs day kay s-tay N L oy-yo)

Do not cut the basket before it's in the hole.
No cortes la cesta bolsa antes de que este en el hoyo.
(no core-tehs la she-stah bole-sah ahn-tehs day K s-tay N L oy-yo)

Cut the basket before you install it.
Quita la cesta antes de instalarlo.
(kwee-tah lah ces-tah ahn-tays day een-stal-r-loh)

Untie the burlap sack.
Desamarra el saco.
(dehs-mar-rah L sah-coh)

Remove the burlap sack.
Remueve el saco.
(reh-mweh-bay L sah-coh)

Leave the burlap sack on.
Dejale el saco.
(deh-hall-eh L sah-coh)

Score the roots before planting.
Rayar las raices antes de plantar.
(rye-ahr lahs rye-sehs ahn-tehs day plahn-tar)

Make it level with the ground.
Nivelalo iqual con el suela / piso.
(nee-beh-lah-low e-kwahl cone L sway-lah / p-soh)

Raise it (3) inches above the ground level.
Subelo (tres) pulgadas sobre el suelo/piso.
(soo-beh-loh (trace) pool-gah-thas so-bray L sway-low / p-soh)

Stagger these plants.
Pon las plantas en forma de zig-zag.
(pone lahs plahn-tahs N fohr-mah day sig-sahg)

Make sure this row is straight.
Asegurate que esta linea este derecha.
(ah-say-goo-rah-tay K s-tah leen-e-ah s-tay deh-reh-cha)

Check it with a level.
Chequealo con el nivelador.
(cheh-k-ah-lo cone L nih-beh-lah-door)

Ask for help when installing this.
Pide ayuda cuando instales esto.
(P-day I-you-dah kwan-doh een-stahl-ehs s-toe)

It's too heavy.
Esto es muy pesado.
(s-toe S moo-e peh-sah-tho)

This is a (3) man job.
Este es un trabajo de (tres) personas.
(s-tay s oohn trah-bah-hoe day (trace) pehr-sohn-ahs)

Set the plants out before you start digging.
Coloca las plantas afuera antes de empezar a cavar.
(coh-loh-cah lahs plahn-tahs ah-fwer-ah ahn-tehs day eem-peh-sahr ah cah-bahr)

Make sure it will look right before you start digging.
Asegurate de que se vea bien antes de empezar a cavar.
(ah-say-goo-rah-tay day K say b-ah B-N ahn-tays day eem-peh-sahe ah cah-bahr)

Use the same sized plants together.
Usa las plantas del mismo tamaño juntos.
(ooh-sah lahs plahn-tahs dehl meese-moh tah-mahn-yoh hoon-tohs)

Alternate tall plants with short ones.
Alterna las plantas altas con las bajas.
(ahl-tehr-na lahs plahn-tahs ahl-tahs cone lahs bah-has)

Use the big ones here.
Usa las grandes aqui.
(ooh-sah lahs grahn-days ah-key)

Use the small ones here.
Usa las pequeñas aqui.
(ooh-sah lahs peh-kwane-yahs ah-key)

Use the tractor to unload trees.
Usa el tractor para descargar los arboles.
(ooh-sah L tractor pah-rah dehs-cahr-gahr lohs ahr-bol-ehs)

Tie down the load securely.
Aprieta el cargamento con seguridad.
(ah-pree-et-ah L cahr-gah-mehn-toe cone she-goo-re-dahd)

Cover the load with a tarp.
Cubre el cargamento con la lona.
(coo-bray L cahr-gah-mehn-toe cone lah loh-nah)

All the trees are tagged at the nursery.
Todos los arboles son marcados en el vivero.
(toe-dohs lohs ahr-bohl-ehs sone mahr-cah-thos N L b-beh-roh)

Choose the nicest plants / trees at the nursery.
Elige las plantas mas bonitas en el vivero
(ehl-e-hay lahs plahn-tahs mahs boh-nee-tahs N L b-behr-oh)

Don't waste any time.
No desperdicies el tiempo.
(no dehs-pehr-d-c-s L t-m-poe)

Take a break.
Toma un descanso.
(toe-mah oohn dehs-cahn-soh)

Take a break at (3) o'clock.
Toma un descanso a las (tres).
(toe-mah oohn dehs-cahn-soh ah lahs(trace)

Take a break in (30) minutes.
Toma un descanso en trienta minutos
(toe-may oohn dehs-cahn-soh N tree-n-tah mee-noo-toes)

Take a break for (10) minutes.
Toma un descanso por diez minutos.
(*toe-mah oohn dehs cahn-soh poor d-s mee-noo-toes)*

Finish this project before lunch.
Termina el proyecto antes de almorzar.
(tehr-mee-nah L pro-yhect-oh ahn-tehs day ahl-mohr-sahr)

Finish this project before quitting time.
Termina el proyecto antes de que el dia finalize.
(tehr-mee-nah L pro-yhewt-oh ahn-tays day K L dee-ah fee-nahl-e-say)

We have to have this done before the end of the day.
Nosotros tenemos que tener esto terminado antes de que el dia finalize.
(noh-soh-trohs teh-neh-mohs K teh-nair s-toe tehr-mee-nah-doh ahn-tays day K L dee-ah fee-nahl-e-say)

LIGHT MASONRY

Mix the cement in here.
Mezcla el cemento en esto.
(mehs-clah L ceh-mehn-toh N S-toh)

Mix (3) shovels of sand to (1) shovel of cement.
Mezcla (tres) palas de arena y (uno) pala de cemento.
(mehs-clah (trace) pah-lahs day r-a-nah E (ooh-noh) pah-lah day seh-men-toh)

Use more / less water.
Usa mas / menos agua.
(ooh-sah mahs / meh-nohs ahg-wah)

Use more / less cement.
Usa mas / menos cemento.
(ooh-sah mahs / meh-nohs ceh-mehn-toh)

Use more sand / rock.
Usa mas arena / roca.
(ooh-sah mahs r-eh-nah / row-cah)

Use less sand / rock.
Usa menos arena / roca.
(ooh-sah meh-nohs r-eh-nah / row-cah)

This mix is too wet / dry
La mezcla es muy mojado / seco.
(la mes-clah S moo-E moe-hah-doh / ceh-coh)

Add this color to the cement.
Añade este color con el cemento.
(ahn-yah-day s-tay coh-lohr cohn L ceh-mehn-toh)

Mix the color exactly the same every time.
Mezcla el color exactamente igual cada vez.
(mehs-clah L coh-lohr x-akt-ah-men-tay e-gwal cah-dah behs)

Compress the soil first.
Comprimir la tierra primero.
(cohm-pree-meer lah t-air-ah pre-mare-oh)

Pour a level foundation to begin.
Llenalo al nivel de la fundacion para empezar.
(yay-nah-loh ahl nee-behl day la foon-dah-c-ohn pah-rah M-peh-sahr)

Follow this line.
Sigue esta linea.
(see-gueh s-tah lee-nee-ah)

The foundation must be (6) in. wide, (20) in. deep.
La fundacion debe ser (seis) pulgadas de ancho (veinte) pulgadas de profundidad.
(la foon-dah-c-ohn deh-beh sehr (sase) pool-gah-thas day ahn-cho (bain-tay) pool-gah-thas pro-foon-d-dahd)

Start the first course (layer) here.
Empieza el primer capa aqui.
(m-p-a-sah L pree-mare cah-pah ah-key)

Check for level and plumb as you go.
Chequea el nivel y la plumeria cada vez que avances.
(cheh-k-ah L nee-behl E la (ploom-air-e-ah cah-tha behs K ah-bahn-sehs)

Use a string line.
Usa una linea de cuerda.
(ooh-sah ooh-nah lee-nee-ah day kwer-dah)

Make a chalk line to maintain a straight edge.
Marca una linea con la tiza para mantener el borde derecho.
(mar-cah ooh-nah lee-nee-ah cone lah t-sah pah-rah mahn-tehn-air L bohr-day deh-reh-cho)

Use 1X4 wood for form boards.
Usa tablas uno por cuatro para los formas.
(ooh-sah tah-blahs ooh-noh poor kwah-troh pah-rah lohs for-mahs)

Use this wood (pegboard) for round forms.
Usa esta madera (no translation) para formas redondas.
(ooh-sah s-tah mah-dare-ah pah-rah for-mahs reh-dohn-dahs)

Use wood stakes every (3) feet.
Usa las estacas de madera cada (tres) pies.
(ooh-sah lahs s-tah-cahs day mah-dare-ah cah-dah (trace) p-ehs)

Put an expansion joint here.
Coloca la conjuntura de expansion aqui.
(coh-loh-cah lah cone-hune-too-rah day x-pahn-c-ohn ah-key)

Put a control joint here.
Coloca la conjuntura de control aqui.
(coh-loh-cah lah cone-hune-too-rah day cohn-trohl ah-key)

Put an isolation joint here.
Coloca la conjuntura de aislamiento aqui.
(coh-loh-cah lah cone-hune-too-rah day ah-e-slah-me-n-toh ah-key)

Put electrical conduit here.
Coloca los conductores de electricidad aqui.
(coh-loh-cah lohs cohn-duke-tohr-ehs day eh-lekt-riss-e-dahd ah-key)

Put drain tubes in every (8) inches.
Coloca los tubos de drenaje cada (ocho) pulgadas.
(coh-loh-cah lohs 2-bohs day dren-ah-hay cah-dah (o-choh) pool-gah-dahs)

Build a block wall first, then lay the stone.
Construye una pared bloqueadora primero, despues pon las piedras.
(cohn-stroo-hyay ooh-nah pah-red boh-k-ah-door-ah pre-mare-oh, dehs-puehs pone lahs p-a-drahs)

Lay the stone first, and grout later.
Arregla las piedras primero, y coloca el cemento despues.
(r-reg-lah lahs p-a-drahs pre-mare-oh E coh-loh-cah L ceh-men-toh dehs-puehs)

Wet the foundation so that the concrete will adhere.
Moja la fundacion para que el concreto se pegue.
(moe-ha lah foon-dah-c-ohn pah-rah K L cohn-creh-toh say peh-gway)

Make sure the joints are small.
Asegura que las conjunturas sean pequeña.
(ah-ceh-goo-rah K lahs cohn-hoon-too-rahs say-on peh-kwane-yah)

Make sure the joints are equal.
Asegura que las conjunturas sean iguales.
(ah-ceh-goo-rah K lahs cohn-hoon-too-rahs say-on e-gwal-ehs)

Cut the stone to fit tighter.
Corta la piedra para que encaje fuertemente.
(core-tah lah p-a-drah pah-rah K n-cah-hay fwer-tah-men-tay)

Clean your tools as you go.
Limpia las herramientas cuando termines de usarlas.
(leem-p-ah las air-rah-me-n-tahs kwan-tho tehr-mee-nehs day ooh-sahr-lahs)

Clean the seams before they dry.
Limpia las ranuras antes de que se sequen.
(leem-p-ah lahs rah-noo-rahs ahn-tays day K say seh-kwen)

Use a wet sponge or cloth.
Usa una esponja mojada o trapo.
(ooh-sah ooh-nah S-pone-ha moh-ha-dah Oh trah-poh)

The finished wall is (10) courses / (3) feet high.
La pared terminada es (diez) ladrillos (tres) pies de alto.
(la pah-red tehr-me-nah-dah S (D-S) lah-dree-yohs / (trace) p-ehs day ahl-toh)

Don't go more than (3) courses high in one day.
No avance mas de (tres) ladrillos alta en un dia.
(no ah-bahn-says mahs day (trace) la-dree-ohs ahl-tah N oohn d-ah)

It will warp.
Esto se deformara.
(s-toh say deh-fohr-mahr-ah)

It will collapse.
Este se colapsara.
(s-tay say coh-lahp-sah-rah)

Set each course (1) inch back from the course below.
Coloca cada linea de ladrillos una pulgada separada de la anterior.
(coh-loh-cah cah-dah lee-nee-ah day lah-dree-yohs ooh-na pool-gah-dah seh-pah-rah-dah day lah ahn-teer-e-ohr)

Use a (screed) board to make the concrete level with the forms.
Usa una (no translation) tabla para nivelar el concreto con las formas.
(ooh-sah ooh-nah tah-blah pah-rah nee-beh-lahr L cohn-cret-oh cone lahs fohr-mahs)

Wait (2) hours before you texture it.
Espera (dos) horas antes de hacer la textura.
(s-pear-ah (dose) oar-ahs ahn-tehs day ah-sehr lah tek-too-rah)

Use this tool to texture the surface.
Usa esta herramienta para marcar la superficie.
(ooh-sah s-tah air-ah-me-n-tah pah-rah mahr-car lah soo-pehr-fee-see)

Use a steel brush.
Usa un cepillo de acero.
(ooh-sah oohn ceh-p-yoh day ah-sehr-oh)

Use a broom.
Usa una escoba.
(ooh-sah ooh-nah s-coh-bah)

Make sure no water stands on the concrete.
Asegurate de que no haya agua en el concreto.
(ah-ceh-goo-rah-tay day K no I-yah ah-gwah N L cohn-creh-toh)

Use the concrete sealer here.
Usa el sellador de concreto aqui.
(ooh-sah L ceh-yah-door day cohn-creh-toh ah-key)

Acid wash this brick tomorrow.
Usa el ácido de lavar en el ladrillo mañana.
(ooh-sah L ah-c-doh day lah-bahr N L lah-dree-yoh mahn-yah-nah)

Don't acid wash this brick.
No uses el ácido de lavar en este ladrillo.
(no ooh-sehs L ah-c-doh day lah-bahr N s-tay lah-dree-yoh)

Backfill this area.
Llena esta area con la tierra.
(yay-nah s-tah ah-re-ah cohn lah t-air-ah)

CLEAN UP

Place all trash/ debris in the dumpster.
Pon toda la basura / escombros en el basurero.
(pone toe-dah la bah-soo-rah / s-comb-rohs N L bah-soo-rare-o)

Remove all trash / debris.
Remueve toda la basura / los escombros.
(reh-mweh-beh toe-dah lah bah-soo-rah / lohs s-comb-rohs)

Put all trash in the truck.
Pon toda la basura en la truca.
(pone toe-dah la bah-soo-rah N la troo-cah)

Put all trash in the trailer.
Pon la basura en el trailer / carreta.
(pone la bah-soo-rah N L trailer / carr-ret-ah)

Do not use the dumpster for debris.
No use el basurero para los escombros.
(no u-say L bah-soo-rare-oh pah-rah lohs s-comb-rohs)

It costs us more money to use this dumpster.
Esto nos cuesta mas dinero si usamos este basurero.
(s-toe nohs kwes-tah mahs d-nare-oh see ooh-sah-mohs s-tay bah-soo-rare-oh)

Wash this area with the hose.
Limpia esta area con agua.
(leem-p-ah s-tah ah-ree-ah cone ah-gwah)

Do not use water to clean.
No uses agua para limpiar.
(no ooh-sehs ah-gwah pah-rah leem-p-ahr)

Sweep up this area.
Barre esta area.
(barr-ray s-tah ah-re-ah)

Leave extra materials for the owner.
Deja el resto de los materiales al dueno.
(day-ha L rehs-toh day los mah-teer-e-ahl-ehs ahl dwane-yo)

Do not leave any materials behind.
No dejes ningun material atras.
(no dehs-hehs neen-goon mah-teer-e-ahl ah-trahs)

Put all the tools away.
Guarda todas las herramientas.
(gwar-dah toe-dahs las air-rah-me-n-tahs)

Put all the materials away.
Guarda todos los materiales.
(gwar-dah toe-dohs los mah-teer-e-ahl-ehs)

Leave the tools here for tomorrow.
Deja las herramientas aqui para manana.
(day-hah las air-rah-me-n-tahs ah-key pah-rah mahn-yahn-ah)

Separate the useable materials from the trash.
Separa los materiales que usas de la basura.
(she-pah-rah los mah-teer-e-ahl-ehs K u-sahs day la bah-soo-rah).

Don't leave anything behind.
No dejes nada.
(no day-hehs na-tha)

Check everything twice.
Chequea todo dos veces.
(cheh-K-ah toe-doh dos beh-cehs)

Empty the truck when you return to the shop.
Vacia la truca cuando vuelvas a la tienda.
(bah-c-ah la troo-cah kwan-doh bwel-bahs ah la t-n-dah)

Clean everything out of the truck.
Limpia todo en la truca.
(leem-p-ah toe-doh N la troo-cah)

Leave the tools in the truck.
Deja las herramientas en la truca.
(day-hah las air-ah-me-in-tahs N la troo-cah)

Leave the materials in the truck.
Deja los materiales en la truca.
(day-hah lohs mah-teer-e-ahl-ehs N la troo-cah)

Leave the parts in the truck.
Dejas las partes en la truca.
(day-hahs lahs pahr-tays N la troo-cah)

Hose out the truck.
Lava con la manguera la truca
(la-bah cone la mahn-gwer-ah la troo-cah)

Wash the truck when you are finished.
Lava la truca cuando tu haya terminando.
(lah-bah la troo-cah kwan-doh too I-yah tehr-me-nahn-doh)

Wash the tools when you are finished.
Lava las herramientas cuando tu hayas terminando.
(la-bah las air-rah-me-in-tahs kwan-doh too I-yahs tehr-me-nahn-doh)

Check all areas twice.
Revisa todas las areas dos veces.
(reh-b-sah toe-dahs las ah-re-ahs dose beh-sehs)

Wear a hard hat at all times.
Usa el casco todo el tiempo.
(ooh-sah L cahs-coh toe-doh L t-m-poe)

Wear safety glasses at all times.
Usa los lentes de seguridad todo el tiempo.
(ooh-sah lohs lehn-tehs day she-goo-re-dahd toe-doh L t-m-poe)

Use the blower to clean this area.
Usa la sopladora para limpiar esta area.
(ooh-sah la so-plah-door-ah pah-rah leem-p-r s-tah ah-re-ah)

Don't use a blower in this area.
No uses la sopladora en esta area.
(no ush-sehs la so-plah-door-ah N s-tah ah-re-ah)

Place it on a tarp.
Colocato en el plastico.
(coh-lo-cah-toh N L plah-stee-coh)

Protect this area with a tarp.
Protégé esta area con el plastico.
(pro-tay-hay s-tah ah-re-ah cone L plah-stee-coh)

Lock everything everything before you leave.
Cierra todo con cerrojo antes de irte.
(c-air-ah toe-doh cone sehr-roh-ho ahn-tays day ear-tay)

Put everything in the garage.
Coloca todo en el garaje.
(coh-loh-cah toe-doh N L gah-rah-hay)

Put everything in the backyard.
Coloca todo en el patio.
(coh-loh-cah toe-doh N L pah-t-oh)

Don't leave anything overnight.
No dejes nada por la noche.
(no deh-hehs nah-dah poor lah no-chay)

Cover these so they don't get wet.
Cubre esto para que no se moje.
(coo-bray s-toh pah-rah K no say mo-hay)

Place weights on top so the wind doesn't blow it away.
Coloca pesas encima para que el viento no las vuele.
(coh-loh-cah pay-sahs n-c-mah pah-rah K L b-n-toh no lahs bway-lay)

Take these tools, we will need them on another job.
Toma estas herramientas, las necesitaremos en otro trabajo.
(toe-mah s-tahs air-rah-me-n-tahs, lahs neh-seh-c-tah-reh-mohs N oh-troh trah-bah-hoe)

Leave these here, we will use them tomorrow.
Deja esto aqui, lo usaremos mañana.
(day-ha s-toh ah-key, loh ooh-sah-reh-mohs mahn-yah-nah)

Make a list of parts that you will need tomorrow.
Haz una lista de todos los respuestos que necesitaremos mañana.
(ahss ooh-nah lees-tah day toh-dohs lohs rehs-pwehs-tohs K neh-seh-c-tah-reh-mohs mahn-yah-nah)

Notes

Apuntes

(Ah-poon-tehs)

How do you say ________________ in Spanish ?

Cómo se dice ________________ en Español?

(Koe-moe say d-say ___________ en s-pahn-yohl?)

Good Work! Let's keep it up.

Specific phrases for property maintenance.

- **Mowing and Trimming**
- **Pruning**
- **Pest Control**
- **Snow Removal**

MOWING AND TRIMMING

Inspect your equipment before use.
Inspecciona tu equipo antes de usarlo.
(een-spek-c-ohn-ah too eh-keep-oh ahn-tays day ooh-sahr-loh)

Make sure everything looks right before you start it.
Asegura que todo esté bien antes de empezar.
(ah-seh-goo-rah K toh-doh s-tay B-N ahn-tays day m-peh-sahr)

Use the equipment properly.
Usa el equipo apropiadamente.
(ooh-sah L eh-keep-oh ah-pro-pre-ah-dah-men-tay)

Start here.
Empieza aqui.
(m-p-a-sah ah-key)

End here.
Termina aqui.
(tehr-me-nah ah-key)

Finish this area first.
Termina esta area primero.
(tehr-me-nan s-tah ah-re-ah pre-mare-oh)

Follow the supervisor's instructions.
Sigue las ordenes del patron.
(c-gway lahs ohr-den-ehs dehl pah-trohn)

Watch out for sprinkler heads.
Cuidado con las cabezas de agua.
(kwee-dahd-oh cone lahs cah-bay-sahs day ahg-wah)

Mow this area every (10) days.
Corta esta area cada (diez) dias.
(core-tah s-tah ah-re-ah cah-tha (d-s) d-ahs.)

Mow this once a week.
Corta esta una vez por semana.
(core-tah s-tah ooh-nah behs poor seh-mahn-ah)

The blades need to be sharpened.
Las hojillas necesitan ser afilidadas.
(lahs o-he-yahs neh-seh-c-tahn sehr ah-fee-lah-thas)

It's too wet to mow today.
Esta muy mojado para cortar hoy.
(s-tah moo-e moe-ha-tho pah-rah core-tahr oy)

If it rains today we will not mow.
Si llueve hoy no cortaremos el cesped.
(see you-web-eh oy no core-tahr-a-mohs L ceh-sped)

Keep mowing even if it starts to rain.
Sigue cortando el cesped aun si empieza a llover.
(see-gway core-than-doh L ceh-sped auhn m-p-a-sah ah yoh-behr)

Wear eye protection at all times.
Usa los lentes de proteccion todo el tiempo.
(ooh-sah lohs lehn-tays day pro-teck-c-ohn toe-doh L t-m-poe)

He / she will show you how.
El / ella te ensañará como hacerlo.
(L / a-yah tay n-sahn-yahr-ah coh-moh ah-sehr-loh)

Show him or her how it's done.
Muéstrarle a el /ella como hacerlo.
(mwest-rahr-lay ah L / a-yah coh-moe ah-sehr-loh)

Mow in a clean pattern.
Corta el cesped de la mismaforma.
(core-tah L ceh-sped day lah mee-sma-for-mah)

Diagonal
Diagonal
(d-ahg-oh-nahl)

Start on the outside, work your way to the center.
Empieza desde afuera hacia al centro.
(m-p-a-sah dehs-day ah-fwer-ah ah-c-ah ahl cen-troh)

Spread the clippings in the garden.
Esparce el cesped cortado en el jardén
(s-par-say L seh-sped core-tah-doh N L har-den)

Put the clippings in the compost pile.
Coloca el cesped cortado en el pilon organico.
(coh-loh-cah L seh-sped core-tah-doh N L p-lohn or-gahn-e-coh)

TRIMMING

Use the string trimmer.
Usa la cortadora de cuerda.
(ooh-sah lah core-tah-dore-ah day kwer-dah)

Use the power edger.
Usa la cortadora de filos / horillas.
(ooh-sah la core-tah-dore-ah day fee-lohs / or-e-yahs)

Cut it shorter.
Cortalo más corto.
(core-tah-loh mahs core-toh)

That is too short.
Eso es muy corto.
(s-o S moo-e core-toh)

Trim along the fence.
Corto al lo largo de la reja alrededor.
(core-toh ahl loh lar-goh day lah ray-hah ahl-reh-deh-dohr)

Trim along the buildings.
Corta alrededor del edificio.
(core-tah ahl-reh-deh-dohr dehl eh-d-fee-c-oh)

Follow the sidewalk/curb.
Sigue la acera.
(c-gway lah ah-ceh-rah)

Don't start before (8)a.m.
No empieces antes de las (ocho) de la manana.
(no m-p-a-sehs ahn-tays day lahs (o-cho) day lah mahn-yahn-ah)

Finish this area today.
Termina esta area hoy.
(tehr-me-nah s-tah ah-re-ah oy)

Finish this area by lunch.
Termina esta area al almuerzo.
(tehr-me-nah s-tah ah-re-ah ahl ahl-mwer-soh)

Trim before mowing.
Corta las bordes antes de que cortes el cesped.
(core-tah lahs bohr-dehs ahn-tays day K core-tays L ceh-sped)

Mow before trimming.
Corta el cesped antes de que cortes las bordes.
(core-tah L ceh-sped ahn-tays day K core-tehs lahs bohr-dehs)

Use the blower to clean up.
Usa la sopladora para limpiar.
(ooh-sah lah soh-plah-door-ah pah-rah leem-p-ahr)

Use a broom to clean up.
Usa la escoba para limpiar.
(ooh-sah lah s-coh-bah pah-rah leem-p-ahr)

PRUNING

Begin here.
Empieza aqui.
(m-p-a-sah ah-key)

Finish here.
Termine aqui.
(tehr-me-nay ah-key)

Use a ladder.
Use la escalera.
(ooh-say lah s-cahl-air-ah)

Use the lift.
Use el levantador.
(ooh say L leh-bahn-tah-door)

Use a safety harness.
Usa el cinturon de seguridad.
(ooh-sah L seen-too-rohn day seh-goo-re-dahd)

Have you used this equipment before?
Has usado este equipo antes?
(ahs ooh-sah-tho s-tay eh-keep-oh ahn-tehs)

I will demonstrate.
Yo te enseñare.
(yoh tay N-sin-yahr-a)

Use a chainsaw.
Use la motosierra.
(ooh-say lay mo-toh-c-air-ah)

Use the pruners.
Use las tijeras
(ooh-say lahs t-hair-ahs)

Use a handsaw.
Usa la sierra pequeña
(ooh-sah lah c-air-ah peh-kwane-yah)

Always wear a hard hat.
Siempre use el casco.
(c-m-pray ooh-say L cahs-coh)

Always wear safety glasses.
Siempre use los lentes protectores.
(c-m-pray ooh-say lohs lehn-tays pro-tehk-tohr-ehs)

Get someone to hold the ladder.
Busca a alguien para que sostenga la escalera.
(booh-ska ah ahl-ghee-n pah-rah K sohs-tehn-gah lah s-cahl-air-ah)

Don't stand under the tree while they are trimming.
No se pare debajo del arbol mientras ellos esten cortando.
(no say pah-ray deh-bah-hoe dehl ahr-bohl me-n-trahs a-yohs s-tehn cohr-than-doh)

For safety, don't work alone.
Por seguridad, no trabaje solo.
(poor seh-goo-re-dahd, no trah-bah-hay so-loh)

Make as few cuts as possible.
Haz los menos cortes posibles.
(ahs lohs mehn-ohs cohr-tehs poe-c-blays)

Remove very few branches.
Remueve muy pocas ramas.
(reh-mway-bay moo-e poe-cahs rah-mahs)

Always cut behind the split.
Siempre corta detras de la división
(C-M-pray core-tah deh-trahs day lah d-v-c-ohn)

Always cut ahead of the split.
Siempre corta adelante de la división.
(C-M-pray core-tah ah-dehl-ahn-tay day la d-v-c-ohn)

Don't damage the buds.
No dañes los capullos.
(no dahn-yays lohs cah-poo-yohs)

Cut it back to here.
Cortalo hasta aqui.
(core-tah-loh ah-stah ah-key)

Remove all branches touching the roof.
Remueve todas las ramas que toque el techo.
(reh-mway-bay toe-dahs lahs rah-mahs K toh-kway L teh-cho)

Remove all branches touching the building.
Remueve todas las ramas que toque el edificio.
(reh-mweh-beh toe-das lahs rah-mahs K toe-kway L ed-e-fee-c-oh)

Remove all branches touching the power lines.
Remueve todas las ramas que toque las lineas de electricidad.
(reh-mweh-beh toe-das lahs rah-mahs K toe-kway lahs lee-nee-ahs day l-ekt-riss-e-dahd)

Watch out for power lines.
Cuidado con las lineas de electricidad.
(kwee-dahd-oh cone lahs leen-e-ahs day eh-lekt-riss-e-dahd.

Wear gloves at all times.
Usa guantes todo el tiempo.
(ooh-sah gwan-tehs toe-doh L t-m-poe)

Watch how I do it.
Mira como lo hago.
(mee-rah coh-moh loh ah-goh)

Do it this way.
Hazlo de esta manera.
(ahs-loh day s-tah mahn-air-ah)

Just cut off the ends.
Solo corta los extremos.
(soh-loh core-tah lohs x-treh-mohs)

Don't cut too deep.
No cortes tan profundo.
(no core-tays tahn proh-foon-doh)

Just cut it so it's smooth.
Solo cortalo de manera que este liso.
(soh-loh core-tah-loh day mah-nare-ah K s-tay lee-soh)

Don't try to make sculptures.
No trates de hacer esculturas.
(no trah-tays day ah-sehr s-cuhl-too-rahs)

PEST CONTROL

This stuff is very dangerous....be careful.
Esto es muy peligroso....ten cuidado.
(s-toh S moo-e peh-lee-groh-soh....tehn kwee-dahd-oh)

Store all chemicals in a locked cabinet.
Guarde los quimicos en un gabinete con candados.
(gwar-day lohs kee-mee-cohs N oohn gah-b-neh-tay cone cahn-dah-dohs)

Never carry these chemicals in the cab of the truck.
Nunca lleves estos quimicos en la cabina de la truka.
(noon-cah yeh-behs s-tohs key-me-cohs N la cah-b-nah day la troo-cah)

Wash your hands after use.
Lávese sus manos despues de usar.
(lah-beh-say soose mahn-ohs dehs-puehs day ooh-sahr)

Always wear a mask.
Siempre usa una mascara.
(c-m-pray ooh-sah ooh-nah mahs-car-ah)

Store all chemicals in their original container.
Guarda todos los quimicos en el envase original.
(gwar-dah toe-dohs lohs key-me-cohs N L n-bah-say o-ree-he-nahl)

Do not use these chemicals or equipment without proper training.
No uses estos quimicos o esos equipos sin entrenamiento.
(no ooh-sehs s-toes key-me-cohs oh s-ohs eh-kweep-ohs seen n-tren-ah-me-n-toh)

Put chemicals in a new container if there is any damage to the original.
Coloca los quimicos en un nuevo envase si este tiene algun daño.
(coh-loh-cah lohs key-me-cohs N oohn nway-boh n-bah-say C s-tay t-n-a ahl-goon dahn-yoh)

Dispose of properly.
Botelos en lugares apropiados.
(boh-the-lohs N loo-gah-rehs ah-pro-p-ah-dohs)

Clean the sprayer before use.
Limpie el atomizador despues de usar.
(leem-p-a L ah-tohm-e-sah-dohr dehs-pwehs day ooh-sahr)

Check for leaks before use.
Revise por aberturas antes de usar.
(reh-b-say poor ah-behr-too-rahs ahn-tehs day ooh-sahr)

Repair any problems before use.
Repare los problemas antes de usar.
(reh-pah-ray loha proh-blehm-ahs ahn-tays day ooh-sahr)

Mix in a well ventilated area.
Mezcle bien en una area ventilada.
(mehs-clay b-n N oohn-ah ah-re-ah behn-t-lah-dah)

Do not spray during high winds.
No use el atomizador durante ventarrones.
(no ooh-say L ah-toh-me-sah-dohr doo-rahn-tay behn-tahr-roh-nays)

Spray it on evenly.
Rocialo parejo.
(roh-c-ah-loh pah-ray-hoh)

Spray it on lightly.
Rocialo ligeramente.
(roh-c-ah-loh lee-gare-ah-mahn-tay)

Spray it on heavily.
Rocialo fuertemente.
(roh-c-ah-loh fwer-teh-men-tay)

Do not spray near play areas.
No use el atomizador cerca de areas de juego.
(no ooh-say L ah-toh-me-sah-dohr sehr-cah day ah-re-ahs day hoo-a-goh)

Pay attention to the wind direction.
Cuiadao con el dirección de la viento.
(kwee-dahd-oh cone L d-rek-c-ohn day lah b-n-toe)

Cover up any cars that are nearby.
Cubre cualquier carros que esten cerca.
(coo-bray kwal-key-air cahr-rohs K ehs-ten sehr-cah)

Wait (5) hours before re-entering area.
Espere (cinco) horas antes de re-entrar al area.
(s-peh-reh (seen-coh) or-ahs ahn-tays day reh-n-trahr ahl ah-re-ah)

Use flags and markers for treated areas.
Use banderas y marcadores para areas en tratamiento.
(ooh-say bahn-dare-ahs E mahr-cah-door-ehs pah-rah ah-re-ahs N trah-tah-me-n-toe)

Clean equipment thoroughly after use.
Limpie completamente el equipo despues de usar.
(leem-p-a cohm-pleh-tah-mehn-tay L eh-kweep-oh dehs-puehs day ooh-sahr)

Never clean parts by blowing through them.
Nunca limpie partes soplando a traves de ellos.
(noon-cah leem-p-a pahr-tehs soh-plahn-doh a trah-behs day a-yohs)

Use the proper amount of solution to avoid disposal after use.
Use la cantidad apropiada de solución para evitar.
(ooh-say lah cahn-t-dahd ah-pro-p-ah-dah day soh-loo-c-ohn pah-rah eh-b-tahr)

If there is excess solution, use on other areas if possible.
Si tiene un exceso de solución, uselo en otras areas si es posible.
(C t-n-a oohn eck-cess-oh day soh-loo-c-ohn, ooh-she-loh N oh-trahs ah-re-ahs C S poh-c-blay)

Dispose of excess solution properly.
Despoje el exceso de solución apropiadamente.
(dehs-poh-hay L eks-cess-oh day soh-loo-c-ohn ah-pro-pre-ah-dah-men-tay)

Do not use too much chemical in one area.
No use muchos químicos en una sola area.
(no ooh-say moo-chos key-me-cohs N ooh-nah so-lah ah-re-ah)

Rinse empty containers thoroughly.
Enjuague con agua los envases vacios completamente.
(n-wha-gway cone ah-gwah lohs ehn-bah-sehs bah-c-ohs cohm-pleh-tah-men-tay)

Transfer rinse water into sprayer for later use.
Lave con agua dentro del atomizador para usarlo despues.
(lah-bay cone ahg-wah dehn-troh dehl ah-toe-me-sah-door pah-rah ooh-sahr-loh dehs-puehs)

Dispose of empty containers properly.
Despoje los envases vacios apropiadamente.
(dehs-poh-hay lohs N-bah-says bah-c-ohs ah-pro-pre-ah-dah-men-tay)

Spills
Derrames
(deh-rah-mehs)

Use protective equipment when handling spills.
Use equipo protector cuando trabaje con los derrames.
(ooh-say eh-kwee-poh pro-tekt-ohr kwan-doh trah-bay-hay cone lohs deh-rahm-ehs)

Use the rubber gloves.
Usa los guantes de goma.
(ooh-sah lohs gwahn-tays day goh-mah)

Contain spills so they will not spread.
Contenga el derrame asi ellos no se expanderan.
(cohn-tehn-gah L dehr-rah-may ah-see A-yohs no say ehx-pahn-der-ahn)

Clean up spills immediately.
Limpie los derrames inmediatamente.
(leem-p-a lohs dehr-rah-mays een-me-d-ah-tah-men-tay)

Report spills to your supervisor immediately.
Reporte sobre derrames a su supervisor inmediatamente.
(reh-poor-tay so-bray dehr-rah-mays ah soo sooper-b-sohr een-me-d-ah-tah-men-tay)

Towels used to clean chemical spills must NOT be put in the regular garbage.
No coloques los trapos que usastes para limpiar los quimicos en la basura.
(no coh-loh-kways lohs trah-pohs K ooh-sah-stehs pah-rah leem-p-r lohs key-me-cohs N lah bah-so-rah)

Towels used to clean chemical spills must go here.
Los trapos usados para limpiar los quimicos debe ir aqui.
(lohs trah-pohs ooh-sah-dohs pah-rah leem-p-r lohs key-me-cohs deh-beh ear ah-key)

Never cover this container.
Nunca cubras este envase.
(noon-cah coo-brahs s-tay n-bah-say)

Always cover this container.
Siempre cubre este envase.
(c-m-pray coo-bray s-tay n-bah-say)

Keep this container outside at all times.
Manten este envase afuera siempre.
(mahn-tehn s-tay n-bah-say ah-fwer-ah c-m-pray)

It is easier to be careful than to clean it up.
Es más fácil tener cuidado que tener que limpiar.
(s mahs fah-seel teh-nair kwee-dah-doh K teh-nair K leem-p-r)

SNOW REMOVAL

You are on call.
Tu estas a mi llamado.
(too s-tahs ah mee yah-mah-tho)

Everyone is on call.
Todos estan a mi llamado.
(toe-dohs s-tahn ah mee yah-mah-tho)

Meet here at (5) a.m.
Nos encontramos aqui a las (cinco)de la manana.
(nohs ehn-cone-trah-mohs ah-key ah lahs (seen-coh) day lay mahn-yahn-ah)

What is your telephone #?
Cual es tu telefono.
(kwal S too teh-leh-foe-noh)

I will call you.
Yo te llamare.
(yoh tay yah-mahr-eh)

Wear sufficient clothing.
Usa suficiente ropa.
(ooh-sah soo-fiss-e-n-tay ro-pah)

You will shovel today.
Tu escavaras hoy. / Tu usas la pala hoy.
(too s-cah-bah-rahs oy.) / *(too ooh-sahs la pah-lah oy)*

You will plow today.
Tu guartaras la nieve hoy.
(too gwar-tahr-ahs la nee-eh-bay oy)

Do you have friends that can work today / tomorrow?
Tienes amigos que pueden trabajar hoy / manana.
(t-n-ehs ah-me-gohs K pway-dehn trah-bah-har oy / mahn-yahn-ah)

I need (two) shovel guys.
Yo necesito (dos) palas.
(yo neh-seh-c-toh (dose) pah-lahs)

Start here / there.
Empieza aqui / allá.
(ehm-p-a-sah ah-key / ah-yah))

Finish here / there.
Termina aquí / alla.
(tehr-me-nah ah-key / ah-yah)

Clean all sidewalks first.
Limpia todos los aceras primeros.
(leem-p-ah toe-dohs lohs ah-sehr-ahs pre-mare-ohs)

Clean all doorways first.
Limpia todas las portales primero.
(leem-p-ah toe-dahs lahs pohr-tahl-ehs pre-mare-oh)

Use salt to melt the ice.
Usa la sal para derretir la nieve.
(ooh-sah lah sahl pah-rah dehr-reh-teer lah nee-eh-bay)

Don't use salt here.
No uses la sal aqui.
(no ooh-sehs la sahl ah-key)

Follow him / her.
Siguelo / siguela.
(see-gway-loh / see-gway-lah)

Don't / do push the snow into the grass.
No / empujes la nieve hacia el cesped.
(no / eem-poo-hays la nee-eh-bay ah-c-ah L cehs-pehd)

Don't / do push snow into the street.
No / empujes la nieve hacia la calle.
(no / eem-poo-hays la nee-eh-bay ah-c-ah lah cah-yay)

Take a break to warm up.
Toma un descanso para calentarte.
(toe-mah oohn dehs-cahn-soh pah-rah cahl-n-tahr-tay)

Notes
Apuntes
(Ah-poon-tehs)

How do you say _______________ in Spanish ?
Cómo se dice _______________ en Español?
(Koe-moe say d-say __________ en s-pahn-yohl?)

Notes

Apuntes

(Ah-poon-tehs)

How do you say _______________ in Spanish ?

Cómo se dice _______________ en Español?

(Koe-moe say d-say __________ en s-pahn-yohl?)

Body Parts

Lists and questions for injuries.

Don't hurt your ...
No hieras ...
(No e-air-ahs)

Did you hurt your ...
Heriste ...
(Air-e-stay)

Don't cut your ...
No te cortes...
(No tay core-tays)

Did you cut your ...
Te cortaste ...
(Tay core-tah-stay)

Don't burn your ...
No te quemes ...
(No tay k-mays)

Did you burn your ...
Te quemaste ...
(Tay k-mah-stay)

Don't twist your ...
No te tuerzas ...
(No tay twer-sahs)

Did you twist your ...
Te torciste ...
(Tay tore-c-stay)

Don't break your ...
No te rompas ...
(No tay rohm-pahs)

Did you break your ...
Te Rompiste ...
(Tay roam-p-stay)

Can you feel your ...
Te sientes ...
(Tay c-n-tays)

Hair	El Pelo	*(Peh-low)*
Nose	La Nariz	*(Nar-ees)*
Eyes	Los Ojos	*(O-hoes)*
Ears	Las Orejas	*(O-ray-hass)*
Face	La Cara	*(Cah-rah)*
Mouth	La Boca	*(Bow-cah)*
Tongue	La Lengua	*(Leng-wah)*
Teeth	Los Dientes	*(D-n-tehs)*

Neck	El cuello	*(Qway-yo)*
Arms	Los brazos	*(Brah-sohs)*
Hands	Las Manos	*(Mah-nohs)*
Thumb	El Pulgar	*(Pool-gar)*
Fingers	Los dedos	*(Day-doe's)*
Finger Nail	Las Uñas	*(Ooh-nyahs)*
Shoulder	El Hombro	*(Ohm-bro)*
Chest	El Pecho	*(Pay-cho)*
Back	La Espalda	*(S-pall-dah)*
- Upper	La Parte de arriba	*(La par-tay day ah-re-bah)*
- Lower	La Parte de abajo	*(La Par-tay day ah-bah-hoe)*
Stomach	El Estómago	*(S-tow-mah-go)*
Hips	Las Calderas	*(Cahl-dare-ahs)*
Groin	El Ingle	*(Een-glay)*
Leg	La Pierna	*(P-air-nah)*
Knee	La Rodilla	*(Row-d-yah)*
Ankle	El Tobillo	*(Toe-b-yo)*
Foot	El Pie	*(P-a)*
Skin	La Piel	*(P-l)*
Bone	El Hueso	*(Way-so)*
Muscle	El Músclulo	*(Moo-skoo-lo)*

Injury Questions

Do you need a doctor?
Necesitas médico / doctor?
(Neh-seh-c-tahs meh-d-co / doke-tore)

Do you have insurance?
Tienes seguridad?
(T-n-ehs seh-goo-re-dahd)

Are you allergic to any medicines?
Tienes alergia a alguna medicina?
(T-n-ehs ahl-er-hee-ah ah ahl-goo-nah meh-d-c-nah)

Write them down. (medicines)
Escríbelas Aquí.
(S-kree-bay-lahs ah-key)

Write down what happened (in Spanish)
Escribe lo que ocurrió (en español)
(S-cree-bay low k o-coo-re-oh (n s-pahn-yol))

Write down when it happened.
Escribe a qué hora ocurrió.
(S-cree-bay ah k or-ah o-coo-re-oh)

Sign it, Please.
Fírmalo por favor.
(Fir-mah-low pour fah-boor)

Do you need stitches?
Necesitas las cosidas?
(Neh-seh-c-tahs las coe-c-dahs)

Do you have a ride to the hospital?
Hay alguien que te puede llevar al hospital?
(Ay ahl-ghee-n k tay pway-day yay-bar ahl os-p-tahl)

Hold it above your head.
Sujétalo arriba de la cabeza.
(Soo-hay-tah-lo ah-re-bah day la cah-bay-sah)

Keep pressure on it.
Mantén la presión.
(Mahn-tehn la preh-c-ohn)

This will sting.
Esto va a picar.
(S-tow bah ah p-car)

Let's change your bandage.
Vamos a cambiar la venda.
(Bah-mose ah cam-b-r la ben-dah)

Don't touch anything
No toques nada.
(No toe-kays nah-dah)

Are you dizzy?
Estás mareado?
(S-tahs mar-a-ah-doe)

Can you hear me?
Me oyes?
(Me oh-yays)

Does it still hurt?
Te duele todavía?
(Tay dway-lay toe-dah-b-ah)

Can you stand up?
Puedes levantarte?
(Pway-days leh-bahn-tar-tay)

Can you walk?
Puedes caminar?
(Pway-days cah-me-nahr)

How many fingers do you see?
Cuántos dedos ves?
(Kwan-toes day-does behs)

Run it under cold water.
Déjalo bajo agua friá.
(Deh-ha-lo bah-ho ah-gwa free-ah)

Put ice on it.
Pon hielo.
(Pone e-a-low)

Sit down.
Siéntate
(C-n-tah-tay)

Don't Move.
No te muevas.
(No tay mway-bahs)

Lean on me.
Apóyate contra mí.
(Ah-poy-ya-tay cone-trah me)

Breathe deep.
Respira profundamente.
(Reh-spear-ah pro-foon-dah-men-tay)

Try to relax.
Trata de relajarte.
(Trah-tah day reh-la-har-tay)

Wear this all the time.
Lleva esto todo el tiempo.
(Yea-bah s-toe toe-doe 1 t-m-poe)

I need the paperwork from the hospital.
Nesecito los papeles del hospital.
(Neh-seh-c-toe los pah-pel-ehs del os-p-tahl).

What is your doctor's name?
Cómo se llama tu doctor?
(Co-moe say yah-mah too doke-tore)

First Aid Kit
Botiquín
(Bow-t-keen)

Band-Aid®
Curita
(Coo-ree-tah)

Gauze
Gasa
(Gasa)

Ointment
Crema curativa
(Cray-mah coo-rah-t-bah)

Hydrogen Peroxide
Peróxido hidrógeno
(Pear-ox-e-doe e-drow-hen-o)

Splint
Tablilla
(Tah-blee-yah)

Tape
Cinta
(Seen-tah)

Cotton
Algodón
(Ahl-go-dohn)

Ice Pack
Compresa de hielo
(Come-preh-sah day e-a-low)

Notes

Apuntes

(Ah-poon-tehs)

How do you say _______________ in Spanish ?

Cómo se dice _______________ en Español?

(Koe-moe say d-say __________ *en s-pahn-yohl?)*

Notes
Apuntes
(Ah-poon-tehs)

How do you say _______________ in Spanish ?
Cómo se dice _______________ en Español?
(Koe-moe say d-say __________ en s-pahn-yohl?)

THE GOOD WORD

Index of key words

Remember:

- **V's** are pronounced like very soft **B's**
- **D's** that aren't the first letter of a word are so soft, they sound like a drunk **"Th"**
- **LL's** sound like **"yeh"**

For more tips on pronunciation, go back to "School" on page 1

A little	Un poco	*oohn poe-coe*
A lot	Mucho	*moo-choe*
Above	Encima	*n-c-mah*
Accident	Accidente	*ahk-c-den-tay*
Account (an)	Cuenta	*kwen-tah*
Acid	Ácido	*ah-see-doh*
Across	Atravesaba	*ah-trah-beh-sah-bah*
Adapter	Adaptador	*ah-dahp-dah-door*
Add (to)	Agregar	*ah-greh-gahr*
Add (up)	Sumar	*soo-mahr*
Adhesive	Adhesivo	*ahd-e-c-boh*
Adjust	Ajustar	*ah-hoo-stahr*
Adjustable	Ajustable	*ah-hoo-stah-blay*
Adjustable nozzle	Boquilla ajustable	*boh-key-yah...*
Aerate	Abrir hoyos	*ah-breer oy-yohs*
Aerator	Abridor de hoyos	*Ah-bree-door day oy-yohs*
Afraid	Miedo	*me-a-tho*
After	Después	*dehs-pwehs*
Afternoon	La tarde	*La tahr-day*
Again	Otra vez	*oh-trah behs*
Aggregate	Rocas	*roh-cahs*
Agree	Acuerdo	*ah-kwer-tho*
Air	Aire	*i-ray*
Air compressor	Compresor de aire	*Cohm-press-ohr day I-ray*
Air filter	Filtro de aire	*Feel-troh ...*
Air gun	Pistola de aire	*p-stol-ah day air*

Alcohol	Same as	*English*
Algae	Algas	*ahl-gahs*
Align (to)	Alinear	*Ah-lin-e-ahr*
Aligned	Alineado	*ah-leen-e-ah-tho*
All	Todo	*toe-thoe*
Alley	Callejuela	*cah-yay-hway-lah*
Also	También	*tahm-b-in*
Alternator	Alternador	*ahl-turn-ah-door*
Aluminum	Aluminio	*ahl-oo-me-knee-oh*
Always	Siempre	*c-m-pray*
Amount	Cantidad	*cahn-t-dahd*
Angle	Ángulo	*Ahn-goo-low*
Angry	Enojado	*N-o-ha-doh*
Annuals	Plantas annual	*Plahn-tahs ah-noo-ahl*
Another (diff)	Otro	*o-troh*
Answer	Respuesta	*rehs-pweh-stah*
Antifreeze	Anticongelante	*ahn-tay-cone-hell-ahn-tay*
Any	Algún	*ahl-goon*
Application (job)	Solicitud	*soh-lih-c-tood*
Application (of material)	Aplicación	*ah-plee-cah-c-ohn*
Apply (mat.)	Aplicar	*ah-plee-cahr*
Approximate (to)	Aproximarse	*ah-prahk-c-mahr-say*
Approximately	Aproximadamente	*ah-prahx-e-mahd-ah-men-tay*
Arch	Archo	*r-cho*
Area	Área	*ah-re-ah*
Arrange	Organizar	*Ohr-gahn-e-sahr*

Arrive	Llegar	*yay-gahr*
Asbestos	Same as	*English*
Ash	Fresno	*freh-snow*
Ask	Preguntar	*preh-goon-tahr*
Asleep	Dormido	*dohr-mead-oh*
Asphalt	Asfalto	*ahs-fall-toe*
Asprin	Aspirina	*ahs-peh-reen-ah*
At least	Al menos	*ahl men-ohs*
At most	Lo maximo	*lo mahx-e-mo*
Average	Medio	*meh-the-oh*
Axe	Hacha	*ah-cha*
Back (side)	Trasera	*tra-sehr-ah*
Back brace	Cinturon de soporte	*Seen-2-rohn day so-poor-tay*
Back up (car)	Marcha atrás	*mar-cha ah-trahs*
Backing (mat)	Refuerzo	*reh-fwer-soh*
Backyard	Patio	*Pah-t-oh*
Bad	Malo	*mah-low*
Bag	Bolsa	*bohl-sah*
Balance	Equilibrio	*eh-qwih-lih-bree-oh*
Balcony	Balcón	*bahl-cone*
Ball	Balón	*bah-lone*
Ball valve	Flotador	*flo-tah-door*
Bar	Barra	*barr-rah*
Barrel	Barril	*bah-reel*
Barrier	Barrera	*bah-rare-ah*
Basement	Sótano	*so-tahn-oh*
Bathroom	Baño	*bahn-yoh*
Battery	Batería	*bah-tare-e-yah*
Beam (wood)	Viga	*v-ha*
Beautiful	Bonita	*bow-knee-tah*
Because	Porque	*poor-k*
Bed (flower)	Macizo	*mah-c-soh*

Beer	Cerveza	*sir-vay-sah*
Bees	Abejas	*ah-bay-hahs*
Before	Antes de	*ahn-tehs day*
Begin	Empezar	*m-peh-sahr*
Behind (posit)	Detrás de	*deh-trahs day*
Below	Debajo	*deh-bah-hoe*
Belt	Cinturón	*Seen-too-rohn*
Bench	Banco	*bahn-coh*
Bend (the)	Curva	*coor-bah*
Bend (to)	Doblar	*doh-blahr*
Beneath	Abajo/debajo	*ah-bah-hoe / deh-bah-hoe*
Bent	Doblado	*doh-blah-tho*
Beside	Junto a	*hoo-n-toe ah*
Best	Mejor	*may-hore*
Between	Entre	*n-tray*
Bicycle	Bicicleta	*b-c-cleh-tah*
Bid	Oferta	*oh-fare-tah*
Big	Grande	*grahn-day*
Bigger	Mas Grandes	*...grahn-dehs*
Bi-lingual	Bilingüe	*b-ling-gway*
Birds	Pájaros	*pa-hah-rohs*
Blade	Cuchilla	*coo-chee-yah*
Bleach	Chloro	*clo-roh*
Block (distance)	Cuadras	*qwa-drahs*
Block (flow)	Obstruir	*ohb-stroo-ear*
Block (material)	Bloque	*bloh-kay*
Blower	Sopladora	*So-plah-door-ah*
Blueprint	Anteproyecto	*ahn-tay-pro-yekt-oh*
Board	Tabla	*tah-blah*
Bolt	Cerrojo	*sehr-o-hoe*
Bolt	Perno	*pair-noh*
Bolt (to)	Anclar	*ahn-clahr*

Bond	Lazo	*Lah-soh*
Bond (to)	Pegar / ahderir	*Pay-gar / ahd-eh-rear*
Book	Libro	*lee-broh*
Boots	Botas	*bo-tahs*
Boring	Aburrido	*ah-boo-re-tho*
Boss	Jefe	*heh-fay*
Bottle	botella	*bow-tay-ya*
Bottom	Fondo	*fone-doh*
Boulder	Pedrusco	*peh-droo-scoe*
Boundry	Límite	*lih-me-tay*
Box	caja	*cah-ha*
Brace	Abrazadera	*Ah-brah-sah-dare-ah*
Brake (The)	Freno	*fray-no*
Brake (To)	Frenar	*fray-nahr*
Brake lights	Luces de freno	*loo-sehs day fray-noh*
Brake pad	Pastilla de frenos	*pah-stee-yah day fray-nohs*
Branches	Ramas	*rah-mahs*
Brass	Latón	*lah-tone*
Break (item)	Romperse	*rohm-pear-say*
Break (time)	Pausa	*pau-sah*
Breaker box	La caja de electricidad	*cah-ha day eh-lekt-riss-e-dahd*
Brick	Ladrillo	*lah-dree-yoh*
Brick hammer	Martillo para ladrillos	*mar-t-yoh pah-rah lah-dree-yohs*
Bricklayer	Albañil	*ahl-bahn-yeel*
Bridge	Puente	*pwen-tay*
Bring (to)	Traer	*trah-ear*
Broke (money)	Pelado /sin dinero	*peh-lahd-oh / seen d-nair-o*

Broken	Rota	*row-tah*
Bronze	Bronce	*brohnss*
Broom	Escoba	*s-co-bah*
Brother	Hermano	*air-mahn-oh*
Brush	Cepillo	*ceh-p-yoh*
Brush (to)	Cepillar	*ceh-p-yahr*
Bubbler	Burbujeador	*bur-boo-hay-ah-door*
Bubbles	Burbujas	*bur-boo-hahs*
Bucket	Cubeta/cubo	*coo-bay-tah / coo-boh*
Buckle	Hebilla	*eh-b-yah*
Buckle (fail)	Hundirse	*oohn-deer-say*
Buckle (to)	Ponerte	*poe-nair-tay*
Bud (flower)	Capullo	*cah-poo-yoh*
Bud (tree)	Brote	*bro-tay*
Bufferzone	Zona intermedia	*soh-nah n-tehr-meh-the-ah*
Build	Construir	*cone-stroo-ear*
Bulbs (plants)	Bulbos	*bool-bohs*
Bulldoze	Derribar	*dehr-re-bahr*
Bulldozer	Excavadora	*x-cah-bah-door-ah*
Bump into	Chocar contra	*cho-cahr cohn-trah*
Buried	Enterrado	*n-teer-rah-tho*
Burn (to)	Quemar	*k-mahr*
Burnt	Quemado	*k-mah-tho*
Burnt out	Calcinado	*cahl-c-nah-tho*
Bury	Enterrar	*n-tear-rahr*
Bus	Camión	*cah-me-yohn*
Bushes	Arbustos	*r-boo-stohs*
Busy	Ocupado	*o-coo-pah-tho*
Butter	Mantequilla	*mahn-teh-key-yah*

Button	Botón	*boh-tohn*
Buy	Comprar	*cohm-prahr*
Cable	Cable	*cah-blay*
Calculate	Calcular	*cahl-coo-lahr*
Calm down	Tranquilizar	*trahn-key-lee-sahr*
Can	Lata	*lah-tah*
Can (able)	Puedes tu	*Pway-thays 2*
Can you	Poder	*poe-dare*
Canvas	Lona	*loh-nah*
Cap	Tapon	*tah-pohn*
Cap (hat)	Gorra	*gohr-rah*
Cap (to)	Tapar	*tah-pahr*
Car	Carro	*car-roh*
Cardboard	Cartón	*cahr-tohn*
Careful	Cuidado	*qwee-dah-doh*
Careless	Descuidado	*dehs-kwee-dahd-oh*
Carpet	Moqueta	*moh-kwet-ah*
Carry	Llevar	*yay-bahr*
Cart	Carro	*cahr-roh*
Cart (to)	Cargar	*cahr-gahr*
case	caja / cajón	*kah-ha / ka-hone*
Case	Cajon	*cah-hone*
Cat	Gato	*gah-toh*
Catch-up	Alcanzar	*ahl-cahn-sahr*
Caulk	Goma selladora	*go-mah say-yah-door-ah*
Caution	Cuidado	*kwee-dahd-oh*
Cement	Cemento	*seh-men-toh*
Center (the)	Centro	*cehn-troh*
Center (to)	Centrar	*cehn-trahr*
Chain	Cadena	*cah-deh-nah*
Chain (to)	Encadenar	*n-cah-neh-dahr*

Chainsaw	Motosierra	*moh-toe-c-air-ah*
Chalk	Tiza	*t-sah*
Chalk line	Linea de tiza	*lih-nee-ah day...*
Change	Cambio	*cahm-b-oh*
Channel (rad)	Canal	*cah-nahl*
Channel (to)	Canalizar	*cah-nahl-e-sahr*
Charge (batt)	Pedro	*peh-droh*
Charge (fee)	Cobrará	*co-brahr-ah*
Cheap	Barato	*bah-raht-o*
Cheat	Tramposo	*trahm-poe-soh*
Check ($)	Chequeo	*cheh-k-oh*
Check (to)	Chequear	*cheh-k-r*
Checkered	A quadros	*ah quad-rohs*
Checklist	Lista	*lee-stah*
Chemicals	Químicos	*key-me-cohs*
Chimney	Chimena	*chih-meh-nay-ah*
Chip (to)	Picar	*p-cahr*
Chipped	Desportillado	*dehs-poor-t-ah-doe*
Chips (wood)	Astillas	*ah-stee-yahs*
Chisel (stone)	Cincel	*seen-cehl*
Chisel (To)	Cincelar	*seen-say-lahr*
Chisel (wood)	Escoplo	*s-co-ploh*
Choke	Estártar	*ehs-tar-tahr*
Choose	Elegir	*eh-leh-hear*
Chop	Hachazo	*ah-cha-soh*
Cigarette	Cigarillo	*c-gar-e-yoh*
Circle	Círculo	*sir-coo-low*
Circle (to)	Rodear	*ro-dare*
Circuit (elec)	Circuito	*sir-key-toh*
Circular saw	Sierra circular	*c-air-ah sir-coo-lahr*
City	Ciudad	*c-ooh-dahd*
Clamp (To)	Sujetar	*soo-tay-har*

Clamps	Abrazaderas	*ah-bra-sah-dare-ahs*
Clay	Arcilla	*ahr-c-yah*
Clean (is)	Limpio	*leem-p-o*
Clean (to)	Limpiar	*leem-p-ahr*
Clear	Claro	*clah-roh*
Clear (to)	Quitar	*key-tahr*
Climb	Trepar	*treh-pahr*
Clippers	Tijeras	*t-air-hahs*
Clock	Reloj	*reh-loh*
Clock out	Marcar la tarjeta	*mar-car la tahr-het-ha*
Close (near)	Cerca de	*sir-cah day*
Close (shut)	Cerrar	*seh-rrar*
Closed	Cerrado	*seh-rah-tho*
Clothes	Ropas	*roe-pahs*
Clumsy	Patoso	*pah-toe-so*
Clutch (car)	Embraque	*m-brah-k*
Coarse	Grueso	*groo-a-soh*
Coat (paint)	Una mano de pintura	*Ooh-nah mah-no day peen-2-rah*
Coat (wear)	Saco	*sah-coh*
Coffee	Café	*cah-fay*
Cold	Frio	*free-o*
Collapse	Hundirse	*oohn-deer-say*
Color	Color	*cuh-lore*
Color (To)	Colorear	*cuh-lore-air*
Combine (to)	Combinar	*cohm-v-nahr*
Come here	Venir	*beh-neer*
Common	Común	*cah-moon*
Compact (to)	Compacto	*cohm-pact-oh*
Compactor	Compactador	*Cohm-pact-ah-door*

Company	Compañia	*cohm-pahn-yee-ah*
Complaint	Queja	*k-hah*
Complete	Completo	*cohm-pleh-toh*
Compost	Abono	*ah-bone-oh*
Compress (to)	Comprimir	*Cohm-pree-meer*
Compressor	Compresor	*Cohm-press-or*
Computer	Computadora	*cohm-poot-ah-door-ah*
Concrete	Hormigón / concreto	*or-me-gohn / cohn-cret-oh*
Concrete mixer	Hormigonera	*or-me-go-nair-ah*
Confused	Confuso	*cone-foo-so*
Connect (to)	Conectar	*co-nekt-r*
Connection	Conexión	*co-nehk-c-ohn*
Consistency	Consistencia	*cone-sis-tehn-c-ah*
Consistent	Constante	*cohn-stahn-tay*
Construct (to)	Construir	*cohn-stroo-ear*
Construction	Construcción	*cohn-strook-c-ohn*
Container	Envase	*ehn-bah-say*
	Contaminado	*cohn-tahm-e-nah-thoh*
Continue	Continuar	*cohn-tin-ooh-ahr*
Contract	Contracto	*cohn-tract-oh*
Contractor	Contratista	*cohn-trah-t-stah*
Control panel	Panel de control	*pah-nehl day cohn-trohl*
Control valve	Válvula de control	*Bahl-boo-lah day cohn-trohl*
Cool (temp)	Fresco	*frehs-koe*
Cool (to)	Enfriarse	*n-free-r-say*

Cooler (beer)	Hielera	*e-l-air-ah*
Copper	Cobre	*co-bray*
Cord	Cordón	*cohr-dohn*
Corner (the)	Esquina	*ehs-kwee-nah*
Corner (the)	Rincon	*reen-cone*
Corner (to)	Curva	*coor-bah*
Cornerstone	Piedra angular	*p-a-drah ahn-goo-lahr*
Correct (is)	Correcto	*coh-rect-oh*
Correct (to)	Corregir	*coh-ray-hear*
Corrosive	Corrosivo	*co-roh-***c***-boh*
Cost	Coste	*coh-steh*
Count (to)	Contar	*cohn-tahr*
Coupler	Enganchar	*n-gahn-char*
Course	Curso	*coor-soh*
Court (b-ball)	Pista	*p-stah*
Court (law)	Tribunal	*treh-vu-nahl*
Cousin	Primo	*pree-moh*
Cover	Cubierta	*coo-b-air-tah*
Cover (To)	Cubrir	*coo-breer*
Co-worker	compañero	*cohm-pahn-yare-oh*
Crack	Grieta	*gree-eh-tah*
Crack (to)	Resquebrajarse	*rehs-kway-brah-har-say*
Cracked	Rajado	*rah-ha-tho*
Crazy	Loco	*lo-co*
Crew	Tripulcación	*trih-pool-cah-c-ohn*
Cross (to)	Cruzar	*cru-sahr*
Crunch	Machacar	*mah-cha-cahr*
Crushed	Molido	*mo-lee-doe*
Cry	Llorar	*yoh-rahr*
Curb	Same as	*English*

Curve	Curva	*cur-bah*
Curve (To)	Curvar	*coor-bahr*
Curves	Tuerces	*twer-cehs*
Customer	Cliente	*klee-n-tay*
Cut (is)	Corte	*core-tay*
Cut (to)	Cortar	*core-tahr*
Cut down	Talar	*tah-lahr*
Cycle	Ciclo	*see-cloh*
Daily	Diario	*d-r-e-o*
Dam	Represa	*reh-preh-sah*
Damage	Daño	*dahn-yoh*
Dangerous	Peligroso	*pehl-e-groh-soh*
Dark	Obscuro	*ohb-skoo-row*
Date	Fecha	*feh-chah*
Day	Día	*dee-ah*
Day off	Dia libre	*d-ah lee-bray*
Deadbolt	Pestillo	*pehs-t-yoh*
Decide	Decidir	*deh-seh-deer*
Deck	Terraza	*teh-rah-sah*
Decorate	Decorar	*deh-coh-rahr*
Deep	Profundo	*pro-foon-doh*
Deeper	Mas profundo	*Mas......*
Degree	Grado	*grah-thoe*
Delicate	Delicado	*dehl-e-cah-thoe*
Delivery	Entrega	*n-tray-gah*
Demolish	Demoler	*deh-moe-lehr*
Demonstrate	Demostrar	*dih-moe-strahr*
Depth	Profundidad	*pro-foon-dee-dahd*
Desk	Escritorio	*s-kree-tohr-e-oh*
Destroy	Destruir	*dehs-true-ear*
Diameter	Diámetro	*d-ah-meht-roh*
Diesel	Gasóleo	*gahs-**o**-lee-oh*
Different	Diferente	*dih-fer-n-tay*

Difficult	Difícil	*deh-feh-seal*
Dig	Excavar	*x-cah-bahr*
Direction	Direccíon	*d-rec-c-ohn*
Dirt	Tierra	*t-air-ah*
Dirty	Sucio	*soo-c-oh*
Dispose	Eliminar	*ih-lihm-n-ahr*
Dissolve	Disolver	*dihs-all-behr*
Distance	Distancia	*dees-tahn-c-ah*
Ditch	Zanja	*sahn-ha*
Do	Hacer	*ah-sayer*
Dog	Perro	*peh-roh*
Dollar	Dólar	*doe-lahr*
Dolly	Carrito manual	*cah-ree-toh mahn-ooh-ahl*
Don't	No	*No*
Don't touch	No tocar	*no toe-car*
Done	Terminando	*tehr-me-nan-doh*
Door	Puerta	*puer tah*
Double	Doble	*doh-blay*
Down	Abajo	*ah-bah-ho*
Downstairs	Abajo	*ah-bah-hoe*
Downtown	Centro	*cehn-troh*
Dozen	Docena	*doe-say-nah*
Drag (to)	Arrastrar	*arr-rast-rahr*
Drain	Desagüe	*dehs-ah-gway*
Drain (to)	Drenar	*dreh-nahr*
Drainage	Drenaje	*dren-ah-hay*
Draw (pen)	Dibujar	*d-boo-har*
Drill	Taladro	*tah-lah-droh*
Drill (to)	Taladrar	*tah-lah-drar*
Drink (to)	Beber	*beh-behr*
Drip	Chorrear	*co-cher-rear*
Drip system	Same as	*English*
Drive (to)	Manejar	*mahn-a-har*

Driveway	Camino de entrada	*cah-me-noh day n-tra-dah*
Drop (to)	Cayeron	*kie-yare-ohn*
Drum	Tambor	*tahm-bore*
Drunk	Borracho	*bo-ra-cho*
Dry (to)	Secarse	*seh-cahr-say*
Dry / Dried	Seco	*Say-co*
Dry measure	medida seca	*meh-d-dah say-ka*
Duct tape (grey tape)	Cinta gris	*seen-tah grease*
Dull	Desafilado	*des-ah-fee-lah-doe*
Dump (the)	Vertedero	*behr-teh-dare-oh*
Dump (to)	Tirar	*T -rahr*
Dump truck	Camión de volteo	*Cah-me-ohn day bohl-tay-o*
Dumpster	Basurero	*bahs-ooh-rare-oh*
Dust	Polvo	*pole-boh*
Dust mask	Máscara para polvo	*mahs-car-ah pah-rah pohl-boh*
Dusting	capa fina	*cah-pah fee-nah*
Dusty	Polvoiento	*pole-boh-e-n-toe*
Each	Cada	*cah-tha*
Early	Temprano	*tehm-prah-no*
Earn	Ganar	*gah-nahr*
Earth	Tierra	*t-air-ah*
East	Este	*ehs-tay*
Easy	Fácil	*fah-seal*
Eat	Comer	*co-mair*
Edge	Borde	*bohr-deh*
Edger	Cortadora de bordes	*Core-tah-dore-ah day bohr-dehs*
Edging	Ribete/Borde	*rih-bet-eh / board-eh*

Either	Cualquiera	*kwal-key-air-ah*
Elbow	Codo	*co-thoe*
Electric	Electrico	*eh-lect-re-coh*
Electrical tape	Cinta electrico	*seen-tah l-eck-tree-coh*
Electricity	Electricidad	*eh-lect-rih-c-dahd*
Elevator	Ascensor	*ah-sehn-sohr*
Emergency	Emergencia	*em-er-hen-c-ah*
Emergency brake	Freno de	*Freh-noh day...*
Employ	Emplear	*m-play-r*
Employee	Empleado	*m-play-ah-tho*
Empty	Vacío	*bah-key-oh*
End	Punta / termino	*poon-tah / tehr-me-noh*
End cap	Capa termino	*cah-pah tehr-me-noh*
Engine	Motor	*moe-tohr*
English	Inglés	*een-glehs*
Enough	Bastante	*bah-stahn-tay*
Enter	Entrar	*ehn-trahr*
Entrance	Entrada	*ehn-trah-dah*
Equal	Igual	*e-gwahl*
Equipment	Equipo	*eh-keep-oh*
Estimate	Presupuesto	*prehs-ooh-pwest-oh*
Even	Nivelado	*nee-behl-ah-tho*
Evenly	Uniformemente	*oohn-e-for-meh-men-tay*
Everything	Todo	*to-tho*
Everywhere	Por todas partes	*poor toe-dahs par-tays*
Exact	Exacto	*eck-sahk-toe*
Example	Ejemplo	*eh-hem-ploh*
Except	Excepto	*ehk-sept-oh*

Exhausted	Agotado	*ah-goh-tah-thoe*
Exit	Salida	*sah-lee-tha*
Expensive	Caro	*carro*
Experience	Experiencia	*x-peer-e-n-c-ah*
Expose	Exponer	*x-pone-air*
Exposed	Expuesto	*x-pwehs-toh*
Extension	Extensión	*x-tin-c-ohn*
Extension cord	Cuerda de extensión	*kwer-dah day x-tin-c-ohn*
Exterior	Exterior	*x-teer-e-ohr*
Extra	Same as	*English*
Eye bolt	Ranura de ojo	*Rah-noo-rah day o-ho*
Fabric	Tela	*teh-lah*
Façade	Fachada	*fah-cha-tha*
Facing (is)	Enfrente	*n-frehn-tay*
Fade (will)	Desteñir	*dehs-tehn-year*
Faded	Descolorido	*dehs-coe-low-ree-thoh*
Fair (is)	Justo	*hoo-stoh*
Fake	Falso	*fal-so*
Fall (season)	Otoño	*oh-tone-yoh*
Fall (to)	Caer	*kah-yare*
False	Falso	*fahl-soh*
Fan	Ventilador	*behn-t-lah-dohr*
Fancy	Decorativo	*deh-coe-rah-t-boh*
Far	Lejos	*leh-hohs*
Far	Lejos	*leh-hohs*
Fast	Rapido	*rah-p-doe*
Fasten	Sujetar	*sue-heh-tar*
Fat	Gordo	*gohr-doh*
Feel (touch it)	Tocar	*Toe-car*
Feet (12 in. +)	Pies	*p-a's*
Fence	Cerca valla	*sir-cah / bah-yah*

Fence stretcher	Valla camilla	*bah-yah cah-me-yah*
Fertilize	Fertilizar	*fehr-till-ih-sahr*
Fertilizer	Fertilizante	*fehr-til-ih-sahn-tay*
Few	Pocos	*poe-cohs*
Field	Campo	*cahm-poe*
Fight	Combatir	*cohm-bat-ear*
File (a)	Lima	*lee-mah*
File (to)	Limar	*lee-mahr*
Fill	Llenar	*yeah-nahr*
Filter	Filtro	*feel-troh*
Final	último	*oohl-t-moh*
Find (it)	Encontrar	*en-cohn-trar*
Fine (small)	fino	*fee-noh*
Finish	Terminar	*tehr-me-nahr*
Fire	Fuego	*fway-goh*
Fired	Despedir	*dehs-peh-dear*
Firm	Fuerte	*fwer-tay*
First	Primero	*pre-mare-oh*
Fit (to)	caber	*cah-behr*
Fittings (parts)	Los partes	*Lohs pahr-tehs*
Fixed (perm)	Fijo	*fee-hoe*
Flags	Banderas	*bahn-dare-ahs*
Flagstone	Losa	*lo-sah*
Flame	Llama	*yah-mah*
Flange	Pestaña	*pehs-tahn-yah*
Flashlight	Linterna	*leen-tare-nah*
Flat	Plano	*plah-noh*
Flatbed	Acoplado	*ah-coh-plah-tho*
Flatten	Aplanar	*ah-plahn-r*
Float	Flotador	*flo-tah-door*
Floor	Suelo	*sway-loh*
Flowerbed	Macizo	*mah-c-soh*

Flowerpot	Maceta / tiesto	*mah-ceh-tah / t-s-toe*
Flowers	Flores	*floh-rehs*
Flowing(style)	Suelto	*swell-toh*
Flush (is)	Nivelado	*nee-behl-ah-tho*
Flush (out)	Limpiar con agua	*leem-p-ahr cohn-ah-gwa*
Flux	Flujo	*floo-hoe*
Foam	Espuma	*s-poom-ah*
Fold (to)	Doblar	*doe-blahr*
Foliage	Follaje	*fo-yah-hay*
Food	Comida	*co-me-dah*
Foot (12 in.)	Pie	*p-a*
For	Para / por	*pah-rah/poor*
Foreman	Capataz	*cah-pah-tahs*
Forget	Olvidar	*ohl-b-dahr*
Fork lift	Porta carga	*por-tah car-gah*
Forked	Bifurcarse	*b-foor-car-say*
Form (paper)	Formulario	*for-moo-lahr-e-oh*
Form (shape)	Forma	*for-mah*
Form (to)	Formar	*for-mahr*
Forms	Formas	*for-mahs*
Forward	Adelante	*ah-dehl-ahn-tay*
Foundation	Cimientos	*c-me-n-toes*
Fountain	Fuente	*fwen-tay*
Framing	Enmarcar	*n-mar-cahr*
Free	Libre	*lee-bray*
Fresh	Fresco	*fres-co*
Friction	Rozamiento	*roh-sah-me-n-toe*
Friend	Amigo	*ah-me-go*
From	Donde	*dohn-day*
Front	Frente	*fren-tay*
Front yard	Yarda del frente	*yar-dah dehl fren-tay*

Frost	Escarcha	*s-car-cha*
Frozen	Congelado	*cone-gay-lah-doe*
Fuel filter	Filtro de gasolina	*feel-troh day gahs-o-leen-ah*
Fuel pump	Surtidor de gasolina	*soor-t-door day......*
Full	Lleno	*yeah-no*
Fumes	Humos	*ooh-mohs*
Funnel	Embudo	*ehm-boo-tho*
Fuse	Fusible	*foo-c-blay*
Fuse box	Caja de.....	*cah-hah day*
Gallon	Galón	*gahl-ohn*
Gap	Hueco	*hway-coh*
Garage	Garaje	*gar-ah-hay*
Garden	Jardín	*har-deen*
Gas	Gas	*ghs*
Gas can	Lata de gas	*lh-tah day...*
Gas mask	Máscara antigás	*mahs-car-ah ahnti-gahs*
Gas tank	Tanque de gas	*Tan-kway*
Gate	Puerta	*pwer-tah*
Gate	Portón	*poor-tone*
Gather	Juntar	*hoon-tahr*
Gauge	Indicador	*n-d-cah-door*
Gear (in)	Engranaje	*n-grahn-ah-hay*
Gear (stuff)	Equipo	*e-kweep-oh*
Generous	generoso	*hen-air-oh-so*
Gentle	Delicado	*dehl-e-cah-tho*
Germinate	Germinar	*her-mean-are*
Get (bring)	Conseguir	*cohn-seh-gweer*
Give	Dar	*dahr*
Glass	Vidrio	*bid-re-oh*
Glazed	Vidriado	*bid-re-ah-thoe*
Gloss	Brillo	*bree-yoh*

Gloves	Guantes	*gwahn-tays*
Glue	Pegamento	*peh-gah-men-toe*
Glue (to)	Pegar	*peh-gahr*
Go	Ir	*ear*
Golf course	Campo de golf	*cahm-po day golf*
Good	Bueno	*bway-no*
Good bye	Adios	*ah-thee-ohs*
Grab	Agarrar	*ah-gahr-rahr*
Gradient	Pendiente	*pehn-d-n-tay*
Gradually	Gradualmente	*grahd-oohl-ah-men-tay*
gram	gramo	*grah-moe*
Grass	Pasto / hierba	*pahs-toh/ e-air-bah*
Gravel	Grava	*grah-bah*
Gravel (fine)	Gravilla	*grah-be-yah*
Gray	Gris	*grease*
Grease	Grasa	*grah-sah*
Grind (to)	Moler	*moh-lare*
Grinder	Trituradora	*tree-too-rah-door-ah*
Groove (a)	Ranura	*rah-noo-rah*
Groove (to)	Cortar (cut)	*cohr-tahr*
Groover	Ranurador	*rah-no-rah-door*
Ground (elect.)	Conectar a tierra	*co-neck-tahr ah t-air-ah*
Ground (tex)	Molido	*mo-lee-tho*
Ground (the)	Suelo	*sway-loh*
Ground frost	Escarcha	*s-car-cha*
Group	Grupo	*groo-poe*
Grout	Lechada	*Leh-cha-dah*
Grove	Arboleda	*r-bow-lay-tha*
Guard	Guardia	*gwar-d-ah*
Guess	Conjetura	*cone-heh-toor-ah*

Gum	Chicle	*chee-clay*
Gutters	Canales	*cah-nahl-ehs*
Hacksaw	Sierra para metales	*c-air-ah pah-rah meh-tahl-ehs*
Hail	Granizar	*grahn-e-sahr*
Hair	Pelo	*peh-loh*
Half	Mitad	*me-tahd*
Hammer	Martillo	*mahr-t-yo*
Hammer (To)	Martillar	*mahr-t-yahr*
Handbrake	Freno de mano	*freh-noh day mah-noh*
Handfull	puñado	*poon-yah-doe*
Handle	Tirador / pomo	*t-rah-door / po-moh*
Handsaw	Serrucho	*seh-roo-cho*
Hang	Colgar	*cohl-gahr*
Hangover	Resaca	*reh-sah-cah*
Happy	Feliz	*feh-lees*
Hard	Duro	*doo-row*
Hardhat	Sombrero duro	*sohm-breh-roh......*
Hardware store	Ferretería	*fehr-reht-air-e-ah*
Harness	Aparejo	*ah-pah-reh-ho*
Hat	Sombrero	*sohm-breh-roh*
Haul	Acarrear	*ah-car-a-r*
Have (to)	Tener	*teh-nair*
Hay	Heno	*eh-no*
Head	Cabeza	*cah-beh-sah*
Health	Salud	*sah-lood*
Hear	Oír	*o-ear*
Heat	Calor	*cah-lohr*
Heater	Calentador	*cah-lent-ah-door*
Heavy	Pesado	*peh-sah-doe*
Height	Altura	*ahl-too-rah*

Hello	Hola	*oh-lah*
Helmet	Casco	*cah-scoe*
Help (to)	Ayudar	*ah-you-thar*
Here	aquí	*ah-key*
Hide	Esconder	*s-cohn-dehr*
High	Alto	*ahl-toe*
Higher	Superior / más alto	*soo-peer-e-or / mahs ahl-toh*
Hill	Colina	*co-lee-nah*
Hinge	Bisagra	*b-sah-grah*
Hire (to)	Contratar	*cohn-trah-tahr*
His	Su	*sue*
Hoe	Azadón	*ah-sah-doan*
Hold this	Sujeta	*Soo-het-ah*
Hole (in object)	Agujero	*ahg-where-oh*
Hole (in soil)	hoyo	*oy-yo*
Holiday	Día festivo	*d-ah fehs-t-boh*
Honest	Honrado	*ohn-rah-thoe*
Hood	Capucha	*cah-poo-cha*
Hook	Gancha	*gahn-cha*
Hook (together)	Enganchar	*n-gahn-char*
Hook up	Conectar	*cone-ect-ahr*
Horn	Claxon	*clahx-ohn*
Hose	Manguera	*mahn-gwair-ah*
Hot	Caliente	*Cahl-e-n-tay*
Hour	Hora	*or-ah*
House	Casa	*cah-sah*
How	Cómo	*coh-moh*
How many	Cuántos	*kwan-tohs*
How much	Cuánto	*kwan-toh*
Humid	Húmedo	*ooh-meh-tho*
Hungover	Crudo	*croo-doe*
Hungry	Hambre	*ahm-bray*
Hurry	Rapido	*rah-p-thoe*

Hurt	Doler	*doh-lare*
I don't know	No se	*no say*
Ice	Hielo	*e-a-low*
Identical	Idéntico	*e-dehn-t-coe*
Ignition	Ignición	*eeg-knee-c-ohn*
Ignore it	Ignorar	*eeg-no-rahr*
Illegal	Ilegal	*e-lee-gahl*
Immigration	Inmigración	*een-me-grah-c-ohn*
Impact head	Cabeza impacto	*cah-bay-sah eem-pact-oh*
Important	Importante	*eem-poor-tahn-tay*
Impossible	Imposible	*eem-poh-c-blay*
Imprint	Sello	*say-yo*
Improve	Mejorar	*may-ho-rahr*
In	En	*in*
Inch	Pulgada	*pool-gah-tha*
Inconsistent	Inconsistente	*Een-cohn-sees-tehn-tay*
Inflate	Inflar	*een-flahr*
Information	Información	*een-for-mah-c-ohn*
Injury	Lesión / herida	*leh-see-ohn / air-e-dah*
Inlaid	Con incrustaciones	*cone een-croo-stah-c-oh-nays*
Insecticide	Insecticida	*en-sekt-e-c-dah*
Inside	A dentro	*ah dehn-troh*
Inspection	Inspección	*in-spec-c-ohn*
Instructions	Instrucciones	*een-strook-c-o-nays*
Insulation	Aislamiento	*i-slah-me-n-toh*
Insurance	Seguro	*seh-goo-roh*

Interior	Interior	*een-teer-e-or*
Interview	Entrevista	*ohn-tray-b-stah*
Into	En	*een*
Invoice	Factura	*fahc-too-rah*
Inward	Hacia dentro	*ah-c-ah dehn-troh*
Iron	Hierro	*e-arrow*
Irrigate	Irrigar	*ear-eh-gahr*
Irrigation	Irrigación	*ear-eh-gah-c-ohn*
Jack	Same as	*English*
Jack up	Levantar	*leh-bahn-tahr*
Jacket	Chaqueta	*cha-ket-ah*
Jail	Cárcel	*cahr-cell*
Jeans	Tejanos	*tay-hahn-ohs*
Job	Trabajo	*tra-ba-hoh*
Joint	Unión	*Oohn-e-ohn*
Joist	Viga	*b-hah*
Joke	Chiste	*chee-stay*
Keep	Guardar	*guar-thar*
Keys	Llaves	*Yah-behs*
Knee	Rodilla	*roh-d-yah*
Knife	Cuchillo	*coo-chee-yoh*
Knob	Perilla	*peh-re-yah*
Knot	Nudo	*new-thoe*
Know (to)	Saber	*sah-behr*
Label	Etiqueta	*eh-t-kweh-tah*
Laborer	Obrero	*o-bray-roh*
Ladder	Escalera	*ehs-calh-air-ah*
Lake	Lago	*lah-goh*
Land	Tierra	*t-air-ah*
Landscape	Paisaje	*pie-sah-hay*
Landscaper	Paisajista	*pah-ee-sah-hee-stah*
Landscaping	ajardinar	*ah-har-d-nahr*
Large	grande	*Grahn-day*

Last	Último	*Oohl-t-moe*
Latch	Pestillo	*peh-stee-yoh*
Late	Tarde	*tar-day*
Law	Ley	*lay*
Lawn	Césped	*ceh-sped*
Lawnmower	Segadura	*segah-doo-ra*
Layer	Capa	*cah-pah*
Layer (to)	Alternar capas	*ahl-ter-nahr cah-pahs*
Lazy	Perezoso /flojo	*peh-reh-soh-soh / flo-ho*
Leak	Gotera	*goh-tear-ah*
Lean (to)	Inclinar	*een-clee-nahr*
Leaning	Inclinada	*een-clee-nah-tha*
Learn	Aprender	*ah-pren-dehr*
Learn	Aprender	*ah-pren-dehr*
Leave	Salir	*sah-leer*
Leave out	Excluir	*x-clue-ear*
Leaves (tree)	Hojas	*o-hahs*
Left	Izquierdo	*is-key-air-doh*
Left handed	Zurdo	*soor-doh*
Leftover	Los restos / Las sobras	*res-toes / so-brahs*
Lend	Prestar	*preh-stahr*
Length	Longitud	*lone-he-tude*
Lengthen	Alargarse	*ah-la-gar-say*
Lengthways	A lo largo	*ah low lar-goh*
Less	Menos	*meh-nohs*
Level (Is)	Llano	*yah-no*
Level (To)	Nivelar	*nee-beh-lar*
Level (tool)	Nivelador	*nee-behl-ah-door*
Lever	Palanca	*pah-lahn-cah*
License	Licencia	*leh-sin-c-ah*
Lift	Levantar	*leh-bahn-tahr*

Light (apply)	Iluminar	*ih-loo-me-nar*
Light (color)	Claro	*clah-row*
Light (elec.)	Luz	*loose*
Light (fire)	Encender	*n-sin-dare*
Light (weight)	Ligero	*lee-gare-oh*
Lighter (Bic®)	Encendedor	*n-sin-deh-door*
Lightning	Relámpago	*reh-lahm-pah-go*
Limb	Rama	*rah-mah*
Limit	Límite	*Lih-mih-tay*
Line	Línea	*lee-knee-ah*
Line level	Linea de nivel	*lee-nee-ah day nee-behl*
Liner	Forro	*for-roh*
Link (chain)	Eslabón	*ehs-lah-bohn*
Liquid	Liquido	*leh-queed-oh*
Liquid measure	Medida Líquida	*meh-d-dah lih-key-dah*
List	Lista	*lee-stah*
Listen	Escuchar	*s-koo-char*
Little	Pequeño	*peh-kwane-yoh*
Live wire	Alambre vivo	*ah-lahm-bray v-boh*
Load (a)	Carga	*car-cah*
Load (to)	Cargar	*car-gahr*
Lock	Cerradura	*cerr-rah-do-rah*
Lock (to)	Cerrar	*cerr-rahr*
Locker	Taquilla	*tah-kwee-yah*
Lock-up	Encerrar	*n-cehr-ahr*
Logs	Troncos	*trohn-cohs*
Long	Largo	*lar-go*
Look at	Mirar	*me-rahr*
Look for	Buscar	*buhs-cahr*
Loose	Suelto	*swell-toe*
Loosen	Aflojar	*ah-flow-har*

Lopper	Same as	*English*
Lose	Perder	*per-dare*
Lost	Perdido	*pear-d-doh*
Loud	Fuerte	*fwer-tay*
Low	Baja	*bah-ha*
Lower (is)	Inferior	*n-fear-e-or*
Lower (to)	Bajar	*ba-har*
Lubricant	Lubricante	*loo-bree-cahn-tay*
Lubricate (to)	Lubricar	*loo-bre-cahr*
Lumber	Madera	*mah-there-ah*
Lunch break	Almuerzo	*ahl-muer-soh*
Machine	Máquina	*mah-key-nah*
Main	Primero	*pree-mare-oh*
Main line	Linea primero	*leen-e-ah......*
Maintenance	Mantenimiento	*mahn-tain-e-me-in-toe*
Make	Hacer	*ah-sehr*
Makeshift	Improvisado	*eem-pro-b-sah-thoe*
Mallet	Mazo	*mah-zoh*
Manager	Gerente	*hair-n-tay*
Many	Muchos	*moo-chohs*
Map	Mapa	*mah-pah*
Marijuana	Mota	*moe-tah*
Mark (to)	Marcar	*mahr-cahr*
Marsh	Pantano	*pahn-tahn-o*
Mask (a)	Máscara	*mahs-car-ah*
Mask (to)	Cubrir	*coo-breer*
Mason (builder)	Mampostero	*mahm-poe-stair-oh*
Masonry	Mampostería	*mahm-poe-stair-e-ah*
Masonry bit	Punta para roca	*poon-tah pah-rah roh-cah*

Master	Maestro	*my-stroh*
Master plan	Plan general	*plahn hen-eh-rahl*
Matches	Fósforos	*fohs-for-ohs*
Matches (same)	Igual	*e-gwahl*
Materials	Materiales	*mah-teer-e-ahl-ehs*
Math	Matemáticas	*mah-t-mah-t-cahs*
Matting	Estera	*eh-stare-ah*
Maximize	Aumentar al máximo	*ow-men-tahr ahl.....*
Maximum	Máximo	*mahx-e-moh*
Me	Yo	*yo*
Measure (to)	Medir	*meh-deer*
Measurement	Medida	*meh-deed-ah*
Measuring tape	Cinta métrica	*seen-tah meh-tree-cah*
Medium	Medio	*meh-thee-oh*
Melt (to)	Derretir	*deh-reh-teer*
Melted	Fundido	*foon-d-doe*
Mesh (a)	Malla	*mah-yah*
Mesh (to)	Engranar	*n-grah-nahr*
Metal	Metál	*meh-tall*
Meter (dist)	Metro	*meh-troh*
Meter (gas)	Contador	*cohn-tah-dore*
Middle	Medio	*meh-the-oh*
Mile	Milla	*me-yah*
Minimize	Minimizar	*me-nee-me-sahr*
Minimum	Mínimo	*me-nee-moh*
Minus	Menos	*meh-nohs*
Minute (1)	Minuto	*me-noo-toe*
Mistake	Error	*a-roar*
Miter saw	Same as	*English*
Mix (the)	Mezcla	*mehs-clah*
Mix (To)	Mezclarse	*mehs-clahr-say*

Mixed	Mezclado	*mehs-cla-doh*
Mixer	Batidora	*bah-t-door-ah*
Model	Modelo	*moh-dell-oh*
Moist	Húmedo	*ooh-may-doe*
Mold (fungus)	Moho	*moh-hoh*
Mold (shape)	Molde	*mohl-day*
Mold (to)	Moldear	*mohl-day-r*
Money	Dinero	*d-nare-oh*
Mop	Trapeador	*trah-p-ah-door*
Mop (to)	Trapear	*trah-p-ahr*
More	Más	*mahs*
More or less	Mas o menos	*mahs O may-nohs*
Mortar	Mortero	*more-tear-o*
Mortarboard	Birrete	*bih-reh-teh*
Mosquitos	Zancudos	*sahn-coo-thohs*
Mountain	Montaña	*mohn-tahn-ya*
Move	Moverse	*moh-bair-say*
Mow	Cortar	*cohr-tahr*
Mower	Cortacésped	*core-tah-seh-sped*
Mud	Barro	*bar-rroh*
Muffler	Silenciador	*c-lehn-c-ah-door*
Mulch	Pajote / mulch	*pah-hoe-tay*
My	Mi	*me*
Nail	Clavo	*clah-boh*
Nail (small)	Puntilla	*poon-t-yah*
Nail (to)	Clavar	*clah-bahr*
Name	Nombre	*nome-bray*
Narrow (is)	Estrecho	*ehs-treh-cho*
Narrow (to)	Reducir	*Reh-doo-seer*
Natural	Natural	*nah-too-rahl*
Natural gas	Gas natural	*gahs na-too-rahl*
Near	Cerca	*sehr-cah*
Necessary	Necesario	*neh-seh-sahr-e-o*
Neck	Cuello	*coo-a-yo*

Need	Necesito	*neh-seh-c-toe*
Needle	Aguja	*ah-goo-ha*
Negative	Negativo	*nay-gah-t-boh*
Neither	Ninguno	*neen-goo-no*
Nest	Nido	*knee-thoe*
Netting	Malla	*mah-yah*
Neutral	Neutro	*nay-ooh-troe*
Neutral (in)	Punto muerto	*poon-toe mwer-toe*
Never	Nunca	*noon-cah*
New	Nuevo	*nway-voe*
Next to	Al lado	*ahl la-tho*
Nice	Simpático	*seem-pah-t-coe*
Night	Noche	*no-chay*
Nightmare	Pesadilla	*peh-sah-d-yah*
No	No	*no*
Noise	Ruido	*roo-e-tho*
Noisy	Ruidoso	*Roo-e-tho-so*
None	Ninguno	*neen-goo-no*
North	Norte	*nor-tay*
Not	No	*no*
Note	Nota	*no-tah*
Notebook	Cuaderno	*kwah-dare-no*
Nothing	Nada	*nah-tha*
Now	Ahora	*ah-or-ah*
Nozzle	Boquilla	*bow-key-yah*
Number	Número	*noo-mare-oh*
Nursery	Vivero	*b-bear-oh*
Nut (bolt)	Tuerca	*twer-cah*
Octagonal	Octagonal	*ohk-tahg-o-nahl*
Of	De	*day*
Off	Apagado	*ah-pah-gawd-oh*
Office	Oficina	*oh-fee-c-nah*
Offset	Compensar	*come-pen-sahr*

Oil	Aceite	*ah-say-tar*
Oil (To)	Lubricar	*loo-breh-car*
Oil can	Aceitera	*ah-say-tair-ah*
Oil filter	Filtro de aceite	*feel-troh day..*
Oil pump	Bomba de aceite	*bohm-bah day...*
Old	Viejo	*b-a-hoe*
Older	Mayor	*meh-yore*
On (power)	Encendido	*n-sin-d-doe*
On (top)	En	*in*
One more	Uno más	*Ooh-no mahs*
Only	Solamente	*sohl-ah-men-tay*
Onto	Sobre	*so-bray*
Open (is)	Abierto	*ah-b-air-toh*
Open (to)	Abrir	*ah-breer*
Opener	Abridor	*ah-bree-door*
Opening	Abertura	*ah-behr-too-rah*
Operate	Manejar	*mah-nay-har*
Opposite	Dc cnfrente	*day ehn-fren-tay*
Or	O	*oh*
Order (in)	Orden	*ohr-dehn*
Order (to)	Pedir	*peh-deer*
Organize	Organizar	*ohr-gahn-e-sahr*
Other	Otro	*oh-troh*
Ounce	onza	*ohn-sah*
Our	Nuestro	*nway-stroh*
Out	Afuera	*ah-fwer-ah*
Outlet (elec)	Enchufe	*n-choo-fay*
Outside	Afuera	*ah-fwer-ah*
Over	Encima	*ehn-c-mah*
Overflow	Rebosa	*reh-boh-sah*
Overlap (To)	Superponer	*soop-air-poe-nair*
Owner	Dueño	*duane-yo*
Pace	Ritmo	*reet-moh*

Pack of cigarettes	Paquete de cigarillos	*pah-keh-tay day c-gar-e-yohs*
Packed	lleno	*yeah-no*
Pain	Dolor	*doh-lohr*
Paint	Pintura	*peen-too-rah*
Paint (to)	Pintar	*peen-tahr*
Paint brush	Brocha de pintura	*bro-cha day peen-too-rah*
Paint sprayer	Pistola de pintar	*pee-stoh-lah day peen-tar*
Pair	Par	*pahr*
Pallate jack	Truca levantar	*troo-cah leh-bahn-tahr*
Pallet	Pallet	*pah-leh-tay*
Panel	Panel	*pah-nehl*
Pants	Pantalones	*pahn-tah-loh-nays*
Paper	Papel	*pah-pel*
Paper suit	Traje de papel	*trah-hay day..*
Paperwork	Papeleo	*pah-pay-lay-oh*
Parallel	Paralelo	*pah-rah-lay-loh*
Park (car)	Aparcar	*ah-pahr-car*
Park (play)	Parque	*par-k*
Part	Parte	*par-tay*
Part time	Tiempo parcial	*t-m-poe par-c-ahl*
Paste	Pasta / masa	*pah-stah / mah-sah*
Patch	Parche	*par-chay*
Patch (to)	Tapar / cubrir	*tah-par / coo-breer*
Path	Camino	*cah-me-no*
Patio	Patio	*pah-t-yoh*
Pattern	Dibujo	*d-boo-hoe*

Pavement	Pavimento	*pah-b-mehn-toe*
Pavers (smooth brick)	Losa en el pavimento	*lo-sah N L pahb-e-me-n-toe*
Pay (to)	Pagar	*pah-gahr*
Paycheck	Sueldo	*soo-l-thoe*
Payday	Día de pago	*dee-ah day pah-go*
Peel off	Despegar	*dehs-pay-gahr*
Peg	Estaca	*s-tah-cah*
Pen	Pluma	*ploo-mah*
Pencil	Lápiz	*lah-piece*
Pendulum	Péndulo	*pehn-doo-loh*
Per	Por	*poor*
Percent	Por ciento	*poor c-n-toe*
Perennial	Planta perenne	*plahn-ta peh-rehn-nay*
Perfect	Perfecto	*pehr-fect-oh*
Perforated	Perforar	*pehr-fo-rahr*
Permanent	Permanente	*pear-mah-nin-tay*
Pesticide	Pesticida	*pehs-t-c-dah*
Phone	Teléfono	*teh-leh-fo-no*
Phone (to)	Teléfonear	*teh-leh-fo-nar*
Photocopy	Fotocopia	*fo-to-co-p-ah*
Pick axe	Pico	*p-coh*
Pick up (To)	Recoger	*ray-co-hair*
Picket	Estaca	*es-tah-kah*
Picket (fence)	Estaca	*s-tah-cah*
Piece	Pedazo / pieza	*peh-dah-soh / p-a-sah*
Pile	Montón	*mohn-tone*
Pin (a)	Perno	*pear-no*
Pinch off	Pellizcar	*peh-yees-car*
Pipe	Tuberia	*to-bair-e-ya*
Piping	Tuberías	*too-bare-e-ahs*

Pitchfork	Horca	*orcah*
Pivot (to)	Pivotar	*p-boh-tahr*
Place	Sitio	*c-t-oh*
Place (to)	Poner	*poe-nair*
Plan (the)	Plan	*plahn*
Plan (to)	Planear	*plahn-a-r*
Plank	Tablón	*tah-blown*
Planning	Planificación	*plahn-eh-fe-cah-see-ohn*
Plant (the)	Planta	*plahn-tah*
Plant (to)	Plantar	*plahn-tahr*
Planter box	Caja de flores	*Cah-ha day floh-rehs*
Planting plan	Plan de los arbustos	*plan day lohs ahr-boo-stohs*
Plaster	Yeso	*yay-soh*
Plastic	Plástico	*plah-stee-co*
Plate (metal)	Chapa	*cha-pah*
Playground	Área de juego	*Ah-re-ah day hway-goh*
Please	Por favor	*poor fah-boor*
Plenty	Bastante	*bahs-tahn-tay*
Pliers	Pinzas / alicates	*peen-sahs / ah-lee-cah-tays*
Plow	Arado	*ah-rah-thoe*
Plow (to)	Arar la tierra	*ah-rar la t-air-ah*
Plug (elect)	Enchufe	*n-choo-fay*
Plug (sinks)	Tapón	*tah-pohn*
Plug (to)	Tapar	*tah-pahr*
Plug in	Enchufar	*n-choo-fahr*
Plumb (is)	Plomo	*plo-moh*
Plumb (line)	Plomada	*plo-mah-tha*
Plumb (tool)	Plomador	*plo-mah-door*
Plumber	Plomero	*ploh-mehr-oh*

Plus	Más	*mahs*
Plywood	Contrachapado	*cone-trah-cha-pah-tho*
Pocket	Bolsillo	*bohl-c-yoh*
Point (end)	Punta	*poon-tah*
Point (place)	Punto	*poon-toh*
Point (to it)	Indicar	*n-d-car*
Pointing tool	Herramienta de indicar	*Air-ah-me-n-tah day en-d-cahr*
Poison	Veneno	*beh-neh-noh*
Polish (the)	Lustre	*loose-tray*
Polish (to)	Lustrar	*loose-trahr*
Poly pipe	Tubo negro	*tooh-bo nehg-row*
Pond (artif.)	Estanque	*s-tahn-k*
Pond (natural)	Charca	*char-kah*
Pool	Estanque	*s-tahn-k*
Poor	Pobre	*po-bray*
Porous	Poroso	*poh-roh-soh*
Positive (attitude)	Positivo	*poe-c-t-boh*
Positive (elec)	Positivo	*poe-c-t-boh*
Positive (sure)	Con convicción	*cone cohn-bic-c-ohn*
Post (display)	Exponer	*x-poe-nair*
Post (fence)	Poste	*poe-stay*
Post hole	Ollo de poste	*oy-yo day…*
Post hole digger	Escavadora	*s-cah-bah-door-ah*
Postpone	Posponer	*pohs-pone-air*
Pot (flower)	Tiesto	*t-s-toe*
Pound (lb.)	Libra	*lee-brah*
Pound (to)	Aporrear	*ah-poe-ray-r*
Pour	Verter	*behr-teer*
Powder	Polvo	*pohl-boh*

Powdered	En polvo	*N pole-voe*
Power	Poder	*poh-dare*
Powerful	Poderoso	*poe-thare-oh-so*
Practice (to)	Practicar	*prahk-t-car*
Precise	Preciso	*pray-c-so*
Pre-fab	Prefabricada	*preh-fahb-re-cah-tha*
Prepare	Preparar	*prep-air-are*
Press (to)	Apretar	*ah-pray-tar*
Pressure	Presión	*preh-c-ohn*
Pressure gauge	Manómetro	*mah-no-meht-roh*
Prevent	Impedir	*m-pay-deer*
Price	Precio	*pray-c-o*
Price list	Lista de precios	*lee-stah day pray-c-ohs*
Primer (auto)	Bomba	*ohm-bah*
Primer (paint)	Base pintura	*bah-say pen-too-rah*
Private	Privado	*pree-bah-tho*
Problem	Problema	*proh-blem-ah*
Process (a)	Proceso	*pro-say-so*
Process (to)	Procesar	*pro-say-sahr*
Project (a)	Proyecto	*pro-yekt-o*
Promotion	Promocio ~ n	*Pro-moe-c-ohn*
Propane	Propano	*pro-pahn-oh*
Protect	Proteger	*pro-tay-here*
Protrudes	Sobresalir	*soh-bray-sah-leer*
Prune (To)	Podar	*poh-dahr*
Pruning shears	Podadera	*poh-dah-dare-ah*
Pry (to)	Abrir con una palanca	*ah-breer cone ooh-nah pah-lahn-cah*
Prybar	Palanca	*pah-lahn-cah*
Pull	Jalar	*ha-lahr*

Pump	Bomba	*bome-bah*
Pump (to)	Bombear	*bome-bay-r*
Puncture	Pinchazo	*peen-cha-soh*
Pure	Puro	*poo-roh*
Push	Empujar	*m-poo-har*
Put	Poner	*poe-nair*
Putty	Masilla	*mah-c-yah*
PVC	Tubo blanco	*tooh-bo blahn-co*
Quantity	Cantidad	*cahn-t-dahd*
Quart	cuarto de galón	*kwar-toe day gah-lone*
Questions	Preguntas	*preh-goon-tahs*
Quick	Rapido	*rah-p-thoe*
Quiet	Silencio	*c-lehn-c-o*
Quit	Dejar	*day-har*
Rack	rejilla	*ray-he-yah*
Radio	Radio	*rah-thee-o*
Radius	Radio	*rah-thee-o*
Rag	Trapo	*trah-poh*
Rail (fence)	Barandilla	*bah-rahn-d-yah*
Rail (stairs)	Pasamanos	*pah-sah mah-nohs*
Railing (in yard)	Verja	*vehr-ha*
Rain	Lluvia	*you-be-ah*
Raise	Levantar	*leh-bahn-tar*
Rake	Rastrillo	*rah-stree-yoh*
Rake (To)	Rastrillar	*rah-stree-yahr*
Ramp	Rampa	*rahm-pah*
Ratio	Proporción	*pro-poor-c-ohn*
Razor	Navaja de afeitar	*na-bah-ha day ah-fee-ih-tar*
Read	Leer	*lay-ear*

Ready?	Preparado / listo	*Prep-ah-rah-thoe / lees-toh*
Rear	Atras	*ah-trahs*
Receipt	Recibo / ticket	*reh-c-boh / ticket*
Recycle	Reciclar	*reh-c-clahr*
Redo	Rehacer	*reh-ah-sehr*
Reduce	Reducir	*reh-do-seer*
Reducer	Reducidor	*reh-do-c-door*
Regular	Regular	*reh-goo-lar*
Relax	Relajarse	*reh-la-r-say*
Reliable	De fiar	*day fee-r*
Remember	Recordar	*reh-core-thar*
Remove	Quitar	*key-tar*
Rent	Alquiler	*ahl-qwee-lare*
Repair	Reparar	*reh-par-r*
Repeat	Repetir	*reh-peh-teer*
Repellent	Repelente	*reh-pehl-n-tay*
Replace	Reemplazar	*ray-im-play-sahr*
Reset	Reajustar	*ray-ah-hoo-star*
Respirator	Respirador	*res-p-rah-door*
Rest	Descansar	*dehs-cahn-sahr*
Retaining wall	Retener	*reh-teh-nehr*
Return	Regreso	*reh-greh-soh*
Reuse	Reusar	*reh-ooh-sahr*
Reverse (auto)	Marcha atras	*mar-cha ah-trahs*
Reverse (gen)	Reverso	*reh-behr-so*
Ride (to)	Paseo	*pah-say-oh*
Ridge	Cresta	*crehs-tah*
Right	Derecho	*deh-retch-oh*
Right (correct)	Correcto	*co-rect-o*
Right angle	Ángulo recto	*ahn-goo-loh rekt-oh*
Ring (a)	Aro	*r-o*

Rinse	Enjuagar	*n-wha-gahr*
Rip	Rasgar	*rahs-gahr*
Ripe	Maduro	*mah-doo-row*
Riser	Elevador	*eh-leh-bah-dor*
Rivet	Remache	*reh-mah-chay*
Rock	Roca	*roke-ah*
Rod	Barra	*bar-rah*
Roll (a)	rollo	*roh-yoh*
Roll it	Enrollar	*en-roh-yahr*
Roller	Rodillo	*roh-d-yoh*
Roll-up (to)	Enrollar	*n-roh-yahr*
Roof	Tejado	*tay-ha-tho*
Room	Habitación	*ah-b-tah-c-ohn*
Root	Raíz	*rah-ease*
Rope	Cuerda	*kwer-tha*
Rotor head	Cabeza de rotor	*cah-bay-sah day roh-tore*
Rotten	Podrido	*poe-dree-tho*
Rough	Desigual	*dehs-e-guahl*
Round	Redondo	*reh-dohn-doe*
Rounded	Redondrado	*reh-dohn-drah-thoe*
Row	Fila	*fee-lah*
Rubber	Goma	*go-mah*
Rubber boots	Botas de gomas	*boh-tahs day goh-mahs*
Rubber gloves	Guantes de gomas	*gwahn-tays day goh-mahs*
Rubber mallet	Mazo de goma	*mah-soh day go-mah*
Rules	Regales	*reh-gah-lays*
Run	Correr	*core-rare*
Rusted	Herrumbroso	*air-room-bro-so*
Sack	Saco	*sah-coh*

Safety	Seguridad	*say-goo-re-dahd*
Safety belt	Cinturón de seguridad	*seen-2-rohn day...*
Safety glasses	Gafas de seguridad	*gah-fahs day seh-goo-reh-dahd*
Safety harness	Arreos de seguridad	*ahr-a-yohs day seh-goo-re-dahd*
Safety valve	Valvula de seguridad	*bahl-boo-lah day...*
Salary	Salario	*sah-lah-re-o*
Salt	Sal	*sahl*
Same	Mismo	*meese-moh*
Sand	Arena	*r-a-nah*
Sand (to)	Lijar	*lee-har*
Sandbag	Saco Terrero	*sah-co teh-rare-oh*
Sandpaper	Papel de lija	*pah-pel day le-ha*
Sandstone	Piedra Arenisca	*p-a-drah r-ehn-ees-cah*
Sap	Savia	*sah-b-yah*
Saturate	Saturar	*sah-2-rahr*
Save	Guardar	*gwar-dahr*
Saw	Serrucho	*seh-roo-cho*
Saw (to)	Serrar	*sehr-rahr*
Sawdust	Serraduras	*seh-rah-do-rahs*
Sawz-all	Same as	*English*
Scaffold	Andamio	*ahn-dah-me-oh*
Scale	Escala	*s-cahl-ah*
Scatter	Esparcir	*s-par-seer*
Schedule	Programa / horario	*pro-grah-mah / o-rah-re-oh*
Scissors	Tijeras	*t-air-hahs*
Scrape (to)	Raspar	*rahs-pahr*
Scraper	Raspador	*rahs-pah-door*

Scraps	Pedacitos	*peh-tha-c-tohs*
Screen	Malla	*mah-yah*
Screw	Tornillo	*tohr-knee-yo*
Screw (To)	Atornillar	*ah-tohr-knee-yahr*
Screwdriver	Destornillador	*dehs tohr-knee-ah-dohr*
Scrub	Fregar	*fray-gahr*
Seal (to)	Sellar	*say-yahr*
Sealant	Sellador	*seh-yah-door*
Season	Estación	*eh-stah-see-ohn*
Seasonal	Temporado	*tehm-poh-rah-doe*
Seat	Asiento	*h-c-n-toh*
Seat belt	Cinturón de seguridad	*seen-2-rohn day seh-goo-re-dahd*
Second (#2)	Segundo	*seh-goon-tho*
Second (time)	Segundo	*seh-goon-tho*
See	Ver / vista	*behr / b-stah*
Seed	Semilla	*seh-me-yah*
Seed (to)	Sembrar	*sehm-brahr*
Seep	Filtrarse	*feel-trahr-say*
Seniority (time)	Antigüedad	*ahn-t-gwee-dahd*
Separate (is)	Separado	*seh-par-ah-tho*
Separate (to)	Separar	*seh-pah-rahr*
Sequence	Secuencia	*seh-qwin-c-ah*
Serious	Serio	*seh-ree-yoh*
Serrated	Serrado	*seh-rah-tho*
Set up	Montar	*mohn-tahr*
Sewage system	Alcantarillado	*ahl-cahn-tar-re-yah-tho*
Sewer	Alcantarilla	*ahl-cahn-tar-re-yah*
Shade	Sombra	*some-bra*
Shake	Agitar	*ah-he-tar*
Shape (a)	Forma	*for-mah*

Shape (to)	Formar	*for-mahr*
Sharp	Afilado	*ah-fee-lah-doe*
Shave (to)	Afeitar	*ah-fay-tar*
Shaved	Afeitado	*ah-fay-tah-doe*
Shears	Tijeras	*t-air-has*
Shed	Cobertizo	*co-behr-tease-oh*
Shelf	Repisa	*reh-p-sah*
Shift	Mover	*mo-bare*
Shift (work)	Turno	*toor-noh*
Shine (to)	Brillar	*bree-yahr*
Shoes	Zapatos	*sah-pah-tohs*
Shop (the)	Tienda	*t-n-dah*
Short	Corto	*court-oh*
Shorten	Acortar	*ah-core-tahr*
Shovel	Pala	*pah-lah*
Shovel (To)	Palar	*pah-lahr*
Shredded	Des menuzado	*dez mehn-ooh-sah-doe*
Shredder	Trituradora	*tree-toor-ah-door-ah*
Shrubs	Arbustos	*ahr-boost-ohs*
Shut	Cerrar	*cer-rahr*
Shut Off	Apagar	*ah-pah-gahr*
Sick	Enfermo	*n-fair-moh*
Side	Lado	*lah-thoe*
Sidewalk	Acera	*ah-sehr-ah*
Sideways	De lado	*day lah-tho*
Sift	Tamizar	*tah-me-sahr*
Sign (the)	Signo	*seeg-no*
Sign (to)	Firmar	*fihr-mahr*
Sink	Lavabo	*lah-bah-boh*
Sink (to)	Hundirse	*oon-deer-say*
Sit	Sentarse	*sehn-tar-say*
Size	Tamaño	*tah-mahn-yo*

Slab	Bloque / losa	*blow-k / lo-sah*
Slack	Flojo	*flo-ho*
Slant	Inclinación	*een-clah-nah-c-ohn*
Sleeves	Fundas	*foon-dahs*
Slice	rebanada	*reh-bahn-ah-dah*
Slide (to)	Deslizar	*dehs-lee-sahr*
Slime	Viscoso	*biece-co-soh*
Slip (to)	Resbalarse	*rehs-bahl-r-say*
Slippery	Resbaladizo	*rehs-bahl-ah-d-soh*
Slope	Pendiente	*pen-d-n-tay*
Slow	Lento	*lehn-toe*
Slow down	Desacelerar	*dehs-a-cell-air-are*
Small	Pequeño	*peh-cane-yoh*
Smaller	Más pequeño	*mahs....*
Smart	Inteligente	*n-tell-eh-hen-tay*
Smeared	Untado	*oohn-tah-doe*
Smell	Olor	*o-lore*
Smoke (gen)	Humo	*oh-moe*
Smoke (to)	Fumar	*foo-mahr*
Smooth	Liso	*lee-soh*
Smooth	Suave	*swa-beh*
Smooth (To)	Alisar	*ahl-e-sahr*
Snow	Nieve	*nee-eh-bay*
Snow shovel	Pala de nieve	*pah-lah day nee-eh-bay*
So	Tan	*tahn*
Soak	Remojar	*reh-moe-har*
Soaker hose	Manguera de remojar	*mahn-gwer-ah day....*
Soap	Jabón	*ha-bohn*
Sober	Sobrio	*so-bree-oh*

Socket (elec)	Enchufe	*n-choo-fay*
Sod	Terrón	*ter-rohn*
Soft	Blando / Suave	*blahn-do swah-vay*
Soil	Tierra	*t-air-ah*
Soiled	Manchar	*mahn-char*
Solder (to)	Soldar	*sohl-dar*
Soldering iron	Soldador	*sohl-dah-door*
Solid	Sólido	*so-lee-tho*
Some	Un poco de	*oohn poe-coe*
Sometimes	A veces	*ah beh-cehs*
Soon	Pronto	*prohn-toh*
Sore	Dolorido	*do-lor-e-tho*
Sorry (I'm)	Lo siento	*lo c-n-toe*
Sound	Sonido	*so-knee-tho*
South	Sur	*soor*
Spaced	Espaciar	*s-pah-c-r*
Spade	Pala	*pah-lah*
Spare (items)	Repuesto	*reh-pues-toe*
Sparks	Chispas	*chee-spahs*
Speak	Hablar	*ahb-lahr*
Specific	Específico	*s-p-c-fee-co*
Speed	Velocidad	*beh-lohs-e-dahd*
Speed limit	Limite de velocidad	*lee-me-tay day beh-loss-e-dahd*
Spill	Derramarse	*dehr-rah-mar-say*
Spin it	Girar	*he-rahr*
Spiral	Espiral	*s-p-rahl*
Splinter	Astilla	*ah-stee-yah*
Split	Dividar	*dih-v-dahr*
Split (to)	Partir	*par-teer*
Split level	Dos niveles	*dose nee-behl-ays*
Sponge	Esponja	*s-pone-ha*
Spout	Caño	*cahn-yoh*

Spray (To)	Rociada	*roe-c-ah-tha*
Sprayer	Atomizador	*ah-toe-me-sah-door*
Spread	Extender	*x-tin-dare*
Spring (boing)	Resorte	*reh-sore-tay*
Spring (H2O)	Manantial	*mah-nahn-t-ahl*
Spring (season)	Primavera	*pre-mah-bare-ah*
Sprinkler	Aspersor	*ahs-pear-sohr*
Sprinkler head	Cabeza de aspersor	*Cah-bay-sah day ……*
Square	Cuadrado	*Kwah-drah-doe*
Square (tool)	Herramienta de cuadrado	*air-ah-me-n-tah day…*
Squeeze	Exprimir	*x-pree-meer*
Stack	Montón	*mohn-tohn*
Stack (to)	Amontonar	*ah-mohn-ton-r*
Staggered	Escalonado	*s-cahl-o-nah-tho*
Stain	Mancha	*mahn-cha*
Stainless	Acero inoxidable	*ah-sehr-oh n-ox-e-dahb-le*
Stairs	Escalones	*s-cahl-o-nays*
Stakes	Estacas	*s-tah-kahs*
Stand (up)	Postura	*poe-stoo-rah*
Stand back	Apartarse	*ah-par-tar-say*
Staple	Grapa	*grah-pah*
Staple (to)	Grapar	*grah-pahr*
Start	Empezar	*m-peh-sahr*
Starter	Boton de arranque	*boh-tohn day ahr-rahn-k*
Statue	Estatua	*s-tah-to-ah*
Stay here	Quedarse	*kway-dar-say*
Steal	Robar	*roh-bahr*
Steel	Acero	*ah-sehr-oh*

Steel toe boots	Botas de punto acero	*boh-tahs day poon-toe ah-sehr-oh*
Steep	Escarpado	*s-car-pah-tho*
Steps	Escalones	*eh-scal-oh-nays*
Stick (onto)	Pegarse	*peh-gar-say*
Stick (poke)	Clavar	*cla-bahr*
Stick (wood)	Ramita	*rah-mee-tah*
Sticks out	Sobresalir	*soh-bray-sah-leer*
Sticky	Pegajoso	*peg-a-ho-so*
Stilt	Pilote	*p-low-tay*
Stir	Revuelve	*reh-bwel-bay*
Stomp	Pisar fuerte	*p-sahr fwar-tay*
Stone	Piedra	*p-aid-rah*
Stoned (weed)	Grifo	*gree-foe*
Stop	Alto	*ahl-toe*
Storm	Tormenta	*tohr-mehn-tah*
Straight	Recto	*rehct-oh*
Straighten	Enderezar	*in-dare-eh-sar*
Strap	Correa	*co-ray-ah*
Strap (to)	Sujetar	*soo-heh-tar*
Stream	Arroyo	*r-roy-yo*
Street	Calle	*cah-yeah*
Stretch (to)	Estirar	*ehs-tih-rahr*
Stretcher	Estirador	*s-t-rah-door*
Stretching bar	Barra estiradora	*bah-rah s-t-rah-door-ah*
String	Cordel / cuerda	*core-dehl / kwer-dah*
String line	Linea de cordel	*lee-knee-ah day core-dehl*
String(To)	Encordar	*n-core-dahr*
Strip (of item)	Franja	*frahn-ha*
Strip (to)	Quitar	*key-tahr*

Strong	Fuerte	*Fwer-the*
Stucco	Estuco	*s-2-coe*
Stuck	Atascado	*ah-tahs-cah-tho*
Stump	Tocón	*toh-cohn*
Sturdy	Sólido	*so-lee-tho*
Style	Estilo	*s-t-low*
Submerge	Sumergir	*soo-mare-here*
Summer	Verano	*beh-rah-noh*
Sun	Sol	*sole*
Sunblock	Bronceador	*brohn-say-ah-door*
Sunburn	Quemado	*k-mah-thoe*
Sunglasses	Gafas de sol	*gah-fahs day sohl*
Sunrise	Salida de sol	*sah-lee-dah day sohl*
Sunset	Puesta de sol	*pueh-stah day soul*
Supplies	Suministros	*soo-me-nee-strohs*
Support	Apoyar	*ah-poe-yahr*
Surface	Superficie	*soo-per-fee-c-ah*
Suspend	Suspender	*soo-spen-dare*
Sweat	Sudar	*soo-dahr*
Sweep	Barrer	*bahr-rare*
Swimming pool	Piscina	*p-c-nah*
Swing pipe	Tubo flexible	*too-bo flehx-e-bleh*
Switch	Interruptor	*n-tehr-rupt-ohr*
Switch (jobs)	Cambiar	*cahm-b-r*
System	Sistema	*c-stee-mah*
Table	Mesa	*may-sah*
Table saw	Serrucha de mesa	*seh-roo-cha day...*
Tacks	Tachuelas	*tah-kway-lahs*

Tags	Etiquetas	*eh-t-kweh-tahs*
Take	Tomar	*toh-mahr*
Take apart	Desmontar	*dehs-mohn-tahr*
Talk	Hablar	*ahb-lahr*
Tall	Alto	*ahl-toh*
Tamp (to)	Atacar / apisonar	*ah-tah-cahr / ah-p-sohn-r*
Tamp (tool)	Pisón	*p-sohn*
Tangle	Enredo	*n-reh-tho*
Tank	Depósito	*deh-poe-c-toh*
Tap (h20)	Llave	*yah-bay*
Tap (to)	Golpecito	*gohl-pay-c-toe*
Tape	Cinta	*seen-tah*
Tape (to)	Pegar con cinta	*pay-gar cone seen-tah*
Tape measure	Cinta métrica	*seen-tah meh-tree-cah*
Tar	Brea	*bray-ah*
Tarp	Lona impermeable	*loh-nah ihm-per-me-ah-blay*
Taut	Tenso	*ten-so*
Taxes	Impuestos	*m-pweh-stohs*
Teach	Enseñar	*ehn-sehn-yahr*
Team	Equipo	*eh-kwee-poh*
Teamwork	Trabajo de equipo	*tra-ba-hoe day a-qwee-poe*
Tear (to)	Rasgar	*rahs-gahr*
Teflon® tape	Cinta teflon	*seen-tah ....*
Telephone	Teléfono	*te-leh-phone-oh*
Temperature	Temperatura	*tem-per-ah-too-rah*
Template	Plantilla	*plahn-t-yah*
Tension bar	Barra de tension	*bah-rah-day ten-c-ohn*

Teriffic	Estupendo	*s-2-pen-tho*
Terrace	Terraza	*tehr-rah-sah*
Terraced	Escalonado	*s-cahl-o-nah-tho*
Terrible	Terrible	*tare-e-blay*
Thank you	Gracias	*grah-c-ahs*
That	Ese / esto	*s-a / s-toe*
The	El /la * los/las	*l/la * lohs-lahs*
Them	Ustedes	*ooh-steh-thehs*
There (is/are)	Hay	*I*
There (it is)	Ahí	*ah-he*
Thermometer	Termómetro	*tare-mome-eht-roh*
These	Esto(a)s	*s-toes *s-tahs*
They	Ello(a)s	*a-yohs * a-yahs*
Thick	Espeso	*s-peh-so*
Thicken	Espesarse	*eh-speh-sahr-say*
Thin	Delgado	*del-gah-doe*
Thin (to)	Diluir	*d-loo-ear*
Things	Cosas	*coh-sahs*
Think	Pensar	*pehn-sahr*
Third	Tercero	*ter-sehr-oh*
This	Este(a)	*s-tay *s-tah*
This afternoon	Esta tarde	*s-tah tar-day*
This morning	Esta mañana	*s-tah mahn-yahn-ah*
Thorns	Espinas	*ace-pee-nahs*
Those	Eso(a)s	*s-ohs * s-ahs*
Threaded coupler	Enganchar rosca	*n-gahn-char roh-skah*
Throttle	Válvula reguladora	*bahl-boo-lah reh-goo-lah-door-ah*
Throw away	Tirar	*t-rahr*
Tie (to)	Amarrar / atar	*ah-mahr-rahr / ah-tahr*

Tier	Grada	*gra-tha*
Tight	Ajustado	*ah-hoo-stah-tho*
Tighten	Apretar / tensar	*ah-pray-tar / ten-sahr*
Tile	Baldosa	*bahl-do-sah*
Tiller	Caña del timón	*Cahn-yah del t-mohn*
Tilt (to)	Inclinar	*een-clee-nahr*
Time	Tiempo	*t-m-poh*
Timer	Reloj	*reh-loh*
Tin	Estaño	*s-tahn-yoh*
Tin snips	Tijeras de estaño	*t-hair-hahs day s-tahn-yoh*
Tip (the)	Punta	*poon-tah*
Tire (car)	Goma / rueda	*go-mah / roo-a-tha*
Tired	Cansado	*cahn-sah-thoe*
Today	Hoy	*oy*
Together	Al mismo tiempo	*ahl me-smo t-m-poe*
Toilet	Baño	*bahn-yoh*
Tomorrow	Manaña	*mahn-yah-nah*
Ton	Tonelada	*tohn-eh-lah-tha*
Tonight	esta noche	*s-tah no-chay*
Tool box	Caja de herramientas	*cah-ha day...*
Tools	Herramientas	*air-ah-me in-tahs*
Top	Arriba / encima	*ah-ree-bah / n-c-mah*
Topsoil	Mantillo	*mahn-t-yo*
Torch	Antorcha	*ahn-tohr-cha*
Torn	Roto	*roh-toh*
Toss (to)	Tirar	*t-rahr*
Total	Total	*toe-tahl*

Total (to)	Sumar	*soo-mahr*
Touch	Tocar	*toe-cahr*
Tow	Remolcar	*reh-mohl-car*
Toward	Hacia	*ah-c-ah*
Towel	Toalla	*toe-ah-yah*
Tractor	Same as	*English*
Traffic	Tráfico	*trah-fee-co*
Trailer	Remolque	*reh mohl-kway*
Translation	Traducción	*trah-duke-c-ohn*
Transplant	Transplantar	*trahns-plahn-tahr*
Trash	Basura	*bah-soo-rah*
Tree	árbol	*ahr-bohl*
Tree trunk	Tronco	*trohn-coh*
Triangle	Triángulo	*tree-ahn-goo-loh*
Trick (a)	Truco	*troo-coh*
Trickle	Hilo	*eee-loh*
Trim (border)	Bordes	*bohr-dehs*
Trim (To)	Cortar	*core-tar*
Trimmer	Cortadora	*core-tah-door-ah*
Trimmings	Recortes	*reh-core-tehs*
Trouble	Problemas	*pro-blehm-ahs*
Trowel	Paleta	*pah-lay-tah*
Truck	Truca	*troo-cah*
Trunk (car)	Maletero	*mah-lay-tare-oh*
Trunk (tree)	Tronco	*trohn-coh*
Trust	Confianza	*cone-fee-ahn-sah*
Try it	Tentativa	*tehn-tah-t-bah*
Tuck (to)	Meter	*meh-tehr*
Turf	Césped	*cehs-pehd*
Turn (corner)	Vuelta	*bwel-tah*
Turn (knob)	Vuelta	*bwel-tah*
Turn around	Volverse	*bohl-bear-say*
Turn down	Bajar	*bah-har*

Turn off	Apagar / cerrar	*ah-pah-gahr / sehr-rahr*
Turn on	Encender / abrir	*n-sin-deer / ah-breer*
Turn over	Voltear	*bohl-tay-r*
Turn up	Subir	*soo-beer*
Turpentine	Aguarrás	*Ah-guahr-rahs*
Twig	Ramita	*rah-me-tahs*
Twist	Giro	*hero*
Twisted	Retorcido	*reh-tore-c-doe*
Ugly	Feo	*fay-o*
Unblock	Desatascar	*dehs-ah-tahs-car*
Uncover	Descubrir	*dehs-coo-breer*
Under	Debajo	*deh-bah-hoe*
Underground	Subterráneo	*soob-tare-rahn-e-oh*
Undergrowth	Maleza	*mah-lay-sah*
Underside	Cara inferior	*cah-rah een-fay-ree-ohr*
Understand	Comprende	*cohm-pren-day*
Underwater	Submarino	*soob-mahr-e-noh*
Undo	Desatar / deshacer	*dehs-ah-tar / dehs-ah-sehr*
Uneven	Desigual	*dehs-e-gwahl*
Unfold	Desplegar	*dehs-pleh-gahr*
Unhook	Desenganchar	*dehs-n-gahn-char*
Unique	Único	*ooh-nee-co*
Unit	Unidad	*ooh-nee-dahd*
Unload	Descargar	*dehs-car-gar*
Unlock	Abrir	*ah-breer*
Unplug	Desenchufar	*dehs-een-choo-fahr*
Unreliable	Poco fiable	*poe-co fee-ah-blay*

Unroll	Desenrollar	*dehs een roh-yahr*
Unsafe	Peligroso	*pehl-e-grohs-oh*
Unscrew (cap)	Desenroscar	*dehs-een-rohs-cahr*
Unscrew (drill)	Destornillar	*dehs-tohr-nee-yahr*
Unstable	Inestable	*n-a-stah-blay*
Untangle	Desenredar	*dehs-in-ray-dahr*
Untie	Desatar	*dehs-ah-tahr*
Until	Hasta	*ah-stah*
Unused	Sin usar	*seen ooh-sahr*
Unwind	Desenrollar	*dehs-een-roh-yahr*
Unwrap	Desenvolver	*dehs-een-bohl-behr*
Up	Arriba	*ahr-ree-bah*
Uphill	Ascendente	*ah-sin-den-tay*
Upright	Vertical	*bare-t-cahl*
Uproot	Arrancar	*r-rahn-cahr*
Upside down	Al revés / boca abajo	*ahl reh-behs / bo-cah ah-bah-hoe*
Upstairs	Arriba	*ah-ree-bah*
Us	Nosotros	*noh-soh-trohs*
Use	Uso / Usar	*ooh-soh ooh-sahr*
Used	Usado	*ooh-sah-tho*
Vacuum	Aspiradora	*ah-spear-ah-door-ah*
Vacuum (to)	Pasar la aspiradora	*pah-sahr la…*
Valve	Válvula	*bahl-boo-lah*
Variety	Variedad	*bahr-I-e-dahd*
Varnish	Barniz	*bahr-nees*
Varnish (to)	Barnizar	*bar-nee-sahr*
Veneer	Chapa	*cha-pah*

Vent	Ventilador	*behn-t-lah-door*
Vertical	Vertical	*behr-t-cahl*
Very	Muy	*moo-e*
Vibration	Vibración	*b-brah-c-ohn*
View	Panorama / vista	*pah-no-rah-mah / v-stah*
Vines	Vides	*b-days*
Vinyl	Vinilo	*beh-knee-low*
Visible	Visible	*b-c-blay*
Vocabulary	Vocabulario	*boh-cahb-ooh-lahr-e-oh*
Voltage tester	Medidor de voltage	*meh-d-door-day bohl-tah-hay*
Volts	Voltios	*bohl-t-ohs*
Volume	Volumen	*bohl-ooh-mehn*
Wadding	Relleno	*re-a-noh*
Wait	Espera	*s-pair-ah*
Wait	Esperar	*s-peh-rahr*
Walk	Caminar	*cah-me-nahr*
Wall (outdoor)	Muro/ pared	*moo-roh /pah-red*
Wall off	Seperar con un muro	*seh-peh-rar cone oon mue-rah*
Want	Querer	*keh-rare*
Warm	Tibio	*tih-b-oh*
Warm up	Calentar	*cah-lane-tar*
Warning	Advertencia	*ahd-bear-ten-c-ah*
Wash	Lavar	*lah-bahr*
Wash	Lavarse	*lah-bahr-say*
Washer (metal)	Arandela	*r-on-day-lah*
Washer (rubber)	Juntura	*hoon-too-rah*
Waste (a)	Derroche	*dare-roe-chay*
Watch (time)	Reloj	*reh-loh*
Watch me	Mírame	*mee-rah-may*

Water	Agua	*ahg-wah*
Water (to)	Regar	*reh-gahr*
Water	Bebedero	*beh-beh-dare-oh*
Water main	Cañeriá del agua	*cahn-yare-e-ah del agh-wha*
Waterfall	Cascada	*cahs-cah-tha*
Waterproof	Impermeable	*eem-per-me-ah-blay*
Wax	Cera	*sarah*
Wax (to)	Encerar	*n-sehr-rahr*
We	Nosotros	*noh-soh-trohs*
Weak	Débil	*deh-beel*
Weather	Tiempo	*t-m-poe*
Weeds	Malas hierbas	*mah-lahs e-air-bahs*
Week	Semana	*seh-mahn-ah*
Weekend	Fin de semana	*feen day seh mahn-ah*
Weigh	Pesar	*peh-sahr*
Weight	Peso	*peh-soh*
Weld (to)	Soldar	*sohl-dahr*
West	Oeste	*ohest-eh*
Wet	Mojado	*moe-ha-doe*
What	Qué	*K*
Wheel	Rueda	*roo-a-tha*
Wheelbarrow	Carretilla	*carr-ret-t-yah*
When	Cuándo	*kwan-thoe*
Where	Dónde	*dohn-day*
Which	Cuál	*kwal*
Who	Quién	*key-N*
Whole	Todo	*toe-doe*
Whole thing	todo / entero	*toe-doe / n-tear-oh*
Why	Por Qué	*poor K*

Wide	Ancho	*ahn-cho*
Widen	Ensancharse	*n-san-char-say*
Width	El Ancho / anchura	*L ahn-cho / ahn-choo-roh*
Wind (air)	Viento	*b-n-toh*
Wind (path)	serpentear	*sehr-pehn-tay-ahr*
Wind (spool)	Enrollar	*n-roh-yahr*
Winter	Invierno	*n-b-air noh*
Wipe	Limpia	*leem-p-ah*
Wire	Alambre	*ah-lahm-bray*
Wire cutters	Cortaalambres	*core-tah-ahl-ahm-brays*
With	Con	*cone*
Without	Sin	*seen*
Wood	Madera	*mah-dare-ah*
Word	Palabra	*pah-lah-brah*
Work	Trabajo	*tra-bah-hoe*
Work (to)	Trabajar	*tra-bah-har*
Worms	Gusanos	*goo-sahn-ohs*
Worn	Desgastado	*dehs-gahs-tah-tho*
Worse	Peor	*pay-or*
Worthless	Sin valor	*seen bah-lohr*
Wrap	Envolver	*n-bohl-behr*
Wrench	Llave inglesa	*yah-bay een-glace-ah*
Wring out	Escurrir	*s-coor-rear*
Write	Escribir	*s-creh-beer*
Wrong	Equivocado	*eh-quib-o-cah-thoe*
Yard	Patio	*pah-t-yo*
Yard (3 ft.)	Yarda	*yard-tha*
Year	Año	*ahn-yoh*
Yell	Gritar	*gree-tahr*
Yes	Si	*See*

Yesterday	Ayer	*I-air*
You	Tu / tus	*tooh / tuhs*
You (pl.)	Ustedes	*ooh-stehs-ehs*
You (sing.)	Usted	*ooh-stehd*
Young	Joven	*ho-behn*
Your	Tus	*toose*
Zero	Cero	*say-roh*
Zig-zag	Zig-zag	*sig-sahg*
Zone	Zona	*so-nah*

Notes

Apuntes

(Ah-poon-tehs)

How do you say _______________ in Spanish ?

Cómo se dice _______________ en Español?

(Koe-moe say d-say __________ en s-pahn-yohl?)

Notes

Apuntes

(Ah-poon-tehs)

How do you say _______________ in Spanish ?

Cómo se dice _______________ en Español?

(Koe-moe say d-say __________ en s-pahn-yohl?)

Tables

- **Numbers**
- **Days, months & time**
- **Colors**

Numbers

Numeros

(New-may-rows)

one	uno	*ooh-no*
two	dos	*Dose*
three	tres	*Trace*
four	cuatro	*kwa-tro*
five	cinco	*sink-o*
six	seis	*Sase*
seven	siete	*c-et-eh*
eight	ocho	*oh-cho*
nine	nueve	*nway-bay*
ten	diez	*d-s*
eleven	once	*ohn-say*
twelve	doce	*doe-say*
thirteen	trece	*tray-say*
fourteen	catorce	*Cah-tore-say*
fifteen	quince	*keen-say*
sixteen	dieciséis	*d-s-e sase*
seventeen	diez y siete	*d-s e c-et-eh*
eighteen	diez y ocho	*d-s e oh-cho*
nineteen	diez y nueve	*d-s e nway-bay*
twenty	veinte	*bain-tay*
thirty	treinta	*tray-n-tah*
forty	cuarenta	*kwar-n-tah*
fifty	cincuenta	*sin-kwen-tah*
sixty	sesenta	*say-sen-tah*

seventy	setenta	*say-ten-tah*
eighty	ochenta	*oh-chen-tah*
ninety	noventa	*no-ben-tah*
one hundred	cien	*c-n*
two hundred	doscientos	*dose-c-n-toes*
three hundred	Trescientos	*Trace-c-n-toes*
four hundred	Quatro-cientos	*kwa-trow-c-n-toes*
five hundred	Quinientos	*keen-e-n-toes*
six hundred	Seiscientos	*Sase-c-n-toes*
seven hundred	Setecientos	*Seh-tay-c-n-toes*
eight hundred	Ochocientos	*oh-cho c-n-toes*
nine hundred	Novecientos	*no-bay-c-n-toes*
thousand	Mil	*Meal*
million	millón	*me-yone*
3/4	Tres cuartos	*Trace qwar-tohs*
1/2	un medio	*oohn med-e-o*
1/4	un cuarto	*oohn kwar-toe*

1/8	un octavo	*oohn ohk-tah-boe*
percent	porcentaje	*por-sen-tah-hay*
dollars	dólares	*doe-lah-rays*
cents	centavos	*sen-tah-bohs*

To construct large numbers, qualify the largest denomination first, then work your way down.

Like this:

2,375,041.65

dos millónes, tres cientos mil, setenta y cinco, quarenta y uno y sesenta y cinco.

(dose me-yone-ehs, trace c-n-toes meal, say-ten-tah e sink-o kwar-n-tah e ooh-no e say-sen-tah e sin-co)

Time

Tiempo

(T-m-poe)

Monday	Lunes	*Loo-nehs*
Tuesday	Martes	*Mar-tehs*
Wednesday	Miércoles	*Me-air-co-lays*
Thursday	Jueves	*Hway-base*
Friday	Viernes	*B-air-nays*
Saturday	Sábado	*Sah-bah-doe*
Sunday	Domingo	*Doe-ming-go*
January	Enero	*N-air-oh*
February	Febrero	*Fehb-rare-oh*
March	Marzo	*Mar-soh*
April	Abril	*Ah-breel*
May	Mayo	*MY-oh*
June	Junio	*Hoo-nee-oh*
July	Julio	*Hoo-le-oh*
August	Agosto	*Ah-go-stow*
September	Septiembre	*Sep-t-m-bray*
October	Octubre	*Ohk-too-bray*
November	Noviembre	*No-b-m-bray*
December	Diciembre	*D-c-m-bray*
Day	Día	*D-ah*
Night	Noche	*No-chay*

Military Time	Tiempo Militario	*T-m-poe mih-lih-tah-re-oh*
Second	Segundo	*Say-goon-doe*
Minute	Minuto	*Min-ooh-toe*
Hour	Hora	*Oar-ah*
Week	Semana	*Say-mahn-ah*
Month	Mes	*Mes*
Year	Año	*Ahn-yo*

At (3) O'Clock	A las (tres)	*Ah las* **trace**
At quarter 'till (5;00) **(Use the number of the coming hour)**	A las **(cinco)** menos cuarto.	*Ah las (***seen-coh)** *meh-noss kwar-toe*
At a quarter past (8:00) **(Use the most recent hour)**	A las **(ocho)** y cuarto	*Ah las* **(oh-cho)** *e kwar-toe*
At a half past (2:00) **(Use the most recent hour)**	A las (dos) y media	*Ah-las* **(dose)** *e meh-the-ah*

- When speaking about the 1:00 hour, simply replace the las's with la and make uno, una.

ie. A la una = At 1:00

- When you want to specify a day on which an event will occur, preced that day with “El”.

  ie. El Martes = On Tuesday.

  For plural, change El to Los.
  ie. On Tuesdays = Los Martes.

Colors
Colores
(Co-low-rays)

red	rojo	*row-hoe*
orange	anaranjado	*ah-na-rahn-ha-doe*
yellow	amarillo	*ah-ma-re-yo*
green	verde	*behr-day*
blue	azúl	*ah-sool*
purple	morado	*moe-rah-doe*
pink	rosado	*row-sah-doe*
black	negro	*neh-grow*
white	blanco	*blahn-co*
brown	castaño	*cah-stahn-yo*
grey	gris	*Grease*
silver	color de plata	*co-lore day plah-tah*
gold	color de oro	*co-lore day oar-oh*
- light	claro	*clah-row*
- dark	oscuro	*oh-skoo-row*

Notes
Apuntes
(Ah-poon-tehs)

How do you say _______________ in Spanish ?
Cómo se dice ________________ en Español?
(Koe-moe say d-say __________ en s-pahn-yohl?)

Notes
Apuntes
(Ah-poon-tehs)

How do you say ______________ in Spanish ?
Cómo se dice ______________ en Español?
(Koe-moe say d-say __________ *en s-pahn-yohl?)*

Notes

Apuntes

(Ah-poon-tehs)

How do you say _______________ in Spanish ?

Cómo se dice _______________ en Español?

(Koe-moe say d-say __________ en s-pahn-yohl?)

Notes
Apuntes
(Ah-poon-tehs)

How do you say ______________ in Spanish ?
Cómo se dice ______________ en Español?
(Koe-moe say d-say _________ *en s-pahn-yohl?)*

Empleo
Employment
(em-ploi-mant)

Me llamo ______.
My name is.
(mai *neim* is)

¿Hablas español?
Do you speak Spanish?
(du iu spik e*span*-ich)

Me gustaría llenar una aplicación.
I would like to fill out an application.
(ai wud laik tu fil aut an a-pli-*que*-chon)

Tengo (2) años de experiencia.
I have (two)years experience.
(ai jav (tu) iars ex-*pir*-i-ans)

Trabajé para _____ compañía.
I worked for ___ company.
(ai uorkd for ____ *com*-pa-ni)

Mi récord de conducir está limpio.
My driving record is clean.
(mai *drai*-ving re-cord is klin)

Aquí tiene mis referencias.
Here are my references.
(jiar ar mai *re*-fer-en-ses)

Yo no tomo
I don't drink.
(ai dount drink)

No uso drogas.
I don't do drugs.
(ai dount du drogs)

¿Qué tipo de identificación requiere?
What identification do you require?
(uat ay-den-ti-fi-*que*-shon du iu nid)

¿Necesito licencia de conducir válida?
Do I need a valid drivers license?
(du ai nid ei velid *drai*-vers *lai*-sens)

Tengo licencia de conducir válida.
I have a valid drivers license?
(ai jav ei valid *drai*-vers *lai*-sens)

Necesito cuarenta horas a la semana.
I need 40 hours a week.
(ai nid *for*-ty auers a wik)

¿Hay horas extras?
Is there any overtime?
(is der eni over-taim)

¿Puedo empezar el lunes?
Can I start Monday?
(can ai estart *mon-day*)

¿Cuándo puedo empezar?
When can I start?
(uen can ai estart)

¿Cuándo se termina la temporada?
When does the season end?
(uen das da *si*-son end)

Necesito (2) días de descanso.
I need (two)days off.
(ai nid (tu) deis of)

¿Puedo trabajar todo el año?
Can I work all year?
(can ai uork oll iar)

¿A qué hora empieza el trabajo?
What time does work start?
(uat *taim* das uork estart)

¿A qué hora terminamos?
What time do we quit?
(uat *taim* du gui cuit)

¿A qué hora es el descanso?
What time are breaks at?
(uat taim ar *breiks* at)

¿Cuándo vamos a almorzar?
When do we take lunch?
(uen du gui teik lonch)

¿Cuánto voy a ganar?
How much will I earn?
(jau mach uil ai ern)

¿Pagan horas extras? ¿Cuánto?
Do I get overtime pay? How much?
(du ai get *ou*-ver-taim pei) (jau mach)

¿Pagan una vez a la semana?
Do you pay once a week?
(du iu pei uans a guik)

¿Pagan cada dos semanas?
Do you pay every two weeks?
(du iu pei evri tu guiks)

¿Cuál es el día de pago?
What day is payday?
(uat dei is pei-dei)

¿Me podría dar un adelanto? ¿Cuánto?
Can I receive an advance? How much?
(can ai ri-siv an ad-vans) (jau mach)

¿Proveen seguro?
Is insurance available?
(is in-*chur*-ans a-*vei*-la-bol)

¿Tendré un vehículo para llevar a casa?
Do I get a vehicle to take home?
(du ai get ei vi-je-col tu teik jom)

¿Me puede recoger en la mañana?
Can you pick me up in the morning?
(can iu pic mi ap in da *mor*-ning)

¿Me puede llevar a casa después del trabajo?
Can you drop me off after work?
(can iu drap mi af after guork)

¿Dónde nos vemos mañana?
Where do we meet tomorrow?
(uer du gui mit tu-ma-rrou)

¿Proveerán un celular?
Do I get a cell phone?
(du ai get ei sell fon)

¿Proveerán una radio?
Do I get a radio?
(du ai get ei *rei*-dio)

¿Tiene trabajo para mis amigos?
Do you have work for my friends?
(du iu jav guork for mai frends)

Equipo

Equipment

(i-cuip-ment)

Nunca he usado este equipo.
I have never used this equipment.
(ai jav never iusd dis i-*cuip*-ment)

¿Me puede mostrar cómo se usa esto?
Can you demonstrate how to use this?
(can iu *de*-mon-estreit jau tu ius dis)

Enséñame cómo.
Show me how.
(cho mi jau)

¿Cómo funciona?
How does it work?
(jau das et guork)

Entiendo/ no entiendo.
I do/ don't understand.
(ai du/ dont an-der-e*stand*)

¿Cómo se limpia esto?
How do you clean it?
(jau du iu clin et)

¿Cómo lo prende?
How do you start it?
(jau du ai estart et)

¿Cuánto gas/ aceite?
How much gas/ oil?
(jau mach gas/ oil)

¿Necesita el obturador?
Does it need the choke?
(das et nid da chok)

¿Está lleno?
Is it full?
(is et ful)

Necesita gas/ aceite.
It needs gas/ oil.
(et nids gas/ oil)

¿Dónde está?
Where is it?
(uer is et)

¿Dónde está el seguro?
Where is the safety?
(uer is da *seif*-ti)

Despacio.
Slow down.
(slou *daun*)

Esto parece estár descompuesto/ gastado.
This looks broken/ worn out.
(dis luks *bro*-ken/ guorn aut)

Está quemando demasiado aceite
It's burning too much oil.
(ets borning tu mach oil)
.
Necesita afilarse.
It needs to be sharpened.
(et nids tu bi *charp*-end)

No marcha bien.
It's running badly.
(ets raning badly)

Hace ruidos extraños.
It's making strange noises.
(ets meiking streinj *noi*-ses)

Solo se paró.
It just stopped.
(et yast stapd)

Ni siquiera lo toqué.
I didn't even touch it!
(ai *di*-dent iven tach et)

¿Por qué no prende?
Why won't it start?
(uay uont et estart)

Demolicion

Demolition

(de-mo-li-chon)

¿Dónde empezamos/ acabamos?
Where do we start/ end?
(uer du qui estart/ end)

¿Cuánto debo quitarle?
How much should I remove?
(jau mach chud ai ri-*muv*)

¿Qué herramienta necesito?
What tools do I need?
(uat tuls du ai *nid*)

¿Se guarda esto? ¿Se guardan estos?
Do we save this/ these?
(du gui seiv dis/ di-is)

¿Qué tan hondo?
How deep?
(jau dip)

¿ Qué tan alto?
How high?
(jau jai)

¿Es esto suficiente?
Is this enough?
(is des i-naf)

Necesitamos un tractor/ máquina.
We need a tractor/ machine.
(ui nid ei trac-tor/ ma-chín)

Hay muchas piedras/ mucho cemento aquí.
There are too many rocks/ too much concrete here.
(der ar tu meny raks/ tu mach *con*-crit jir)

Enséñame dónde están las líneas de utilidad.
Show me where the utility lines are located.
(chou mi uer da iu-*ti*-li-ti lains ar *lo*-kei-ted)

¿Dónde pongo la basura/ los despojos?
Where do I put the trash/ debris?
(uer du ai put da trach/ de-bri)

¿Dónde consigo agua?
Where do I get water?
(uer du ai get *gua*-ter)

Seguridad / Lesion

Safety/ Injury

(seif-ti/en-yuri)

Con cuidado.
Be careful.
(bi *ker*-ful)

Necesito…
I need a…
(ai nid ei)

… un casco.
Hard hat
(jard jat)

… unos guantes.
Gloves
(glovs)

… lentes de protección.
Safety glasses
(seif-ti glases)

...tapones para los oídos
Ear plugs
(iar plogs)

Estoy lastimado.
I am injured.
(ai em *in*-yurd)

Me lastimé.
I hurt myself.
(ai jurt mai-*self*)

Me duele.
It hurts.
(et jurts)

Estoy enfermo.
I am sick.
(ai em sick)

Estoy sangrando.
I am bleeding.
(ai em *bli*-ding)

Necesito una venda.
I need a band-aid.TM
(ai nid ei band-eit)

Necesito un doctor.
I need a doctor.
(ai nid ei *doc*-tor)

Me quebré el pie/ brazo/ mano/ dedo.
I broke my foot/ arm/ hand/ finger.
(ai brok mai fut/ arm/ jand/ *fin*-ger)

Hay un derrame químico.
There is a chemical spill.
(der is ei *ke*-mi-cal spil)

¿Cómo puedo limpiarlo sin daños.
How do I clean it up safely?
(jau du ai clin et ap *scif-li)*

Necesito tomar agua.
I need a drink of water.
(ai nid ei drink of *gua*-ter)

Frases General

General Phrases

(yen-er-al frais-es)

Necesito ayuda.
I need help.
(ai nid jelp)

Hay demasiados hombres.
There are too many men.
(der ar tu me-ni men)

No tememos suficiente.
We don't have enough.
(gui dont jav i-naf)

Esta herramienta está quebrada.
This tool is broken.
(dis tul is *bro*-ken)

Esta máquina está quebrada.
This machine is broken.
(dis ma-*chin* is *bro*-ken)

El camión no prende
The truck won't start.
(da truk quont estart)

La máquina no prende.
The machine won't start.
(da ma-*chin* guont estart)

Se le acabó el aceite.
It is out of oil.
(et is aut af oil)

Se le acabó el gas.
It is out of gas.
(et is aut af gas)

El cinturón se quebró.
The belt is broken.
(da belt is *bro*-ken)

Una cabeza/ cuchilla/ herramienta está quebrada.
There is a broken head/ blade/ tool.
(der is ei *bro*-ken jed/ bleid/ *tùl*)

¿Quieres que recoja a José mañana?
Should I pick up Jose tomorrow?
(chud ai pik ap Jose tu-*ma*-rrou)

José se fué a casa y no regresó.
Jose went home and did not come back.
(Jose uent jom end did not com back)

José no vino a trabajar.
Jose did not come to work.
(Jose did not com tu work)

El cliente está enojado.
The client is upset.
(da claient is ap-*set*)

Los materiales nunca llegaron.
The materials never arrived.
(da ma-*tir*-ials *ne*-ver a-*rraivd*)

Vamos retrasados en el trabajo.
We are behind on schedule.
(gui ar bi-*jaind* an e*sked*-yul)

Los planes no están claros.
The plans are not clear.
(da plans ar not clir)

Necesito esta parte.
I need this part.
(ai nid dis part)

Es muy barato/ caro
It's too cheap/ expensive.
(ets tu chip/ ex-*pen*-siv)

Está muy pesado
It's too heavy.
(ets tu jevi)

¿Es el tamaño equivocado?
Is it the wrong size?
(is et da rong sais)

Está muy grande.
It's too big.
(ets tu big)

Está muy chico.
It's too small.
(ets tu esmall)

Está muy corto/ alto.
It's too short/ tall.
(ets tu chort/ tal)

Está muy seco.
It's too dry.
(ets tu drai)

Necesita agua.
It needs water.
(et nids guater)

¿Dónde consigo agua?
Where do I get water?
(guer du ai get *gua*-ter)

Está muy mojado.
It's too wet.
(ets tu guet)

El suelo está muy mojado.
The ground is too wet.
(da graund is tu guet)

Está nevando/ lloviendo.
It is snowing/ raining.
(et is e*sno*-guind/ *rei*-ning)

Golpeamos una línea de utilidad.
We hit a utility line.
(gui hit ei u-*ti*-li-ti lain)

¿Dónde consigo electricidad?
Where do I get electricity?
(guer du ai get e-lec-*tri*-si-ti)

Necesitamos más tiempo.
We need more time.
(gui nid mor taim)

Se hace tarde.
It's getting late.
(ets get-ing leit)

Necesitamos acabar hoy.
We need to finish today.
(gui nid tu *fi*-nisch tu-dei)
.
Necesitamos acabar mañana.
We need to finish tomorrow.
(ui nid tu *fi*-nisch tu-*mar*-ou)

Cuando tememos que acabar?
When do we have to finish?
(guen du ui jav tu *fi*-nisch)

¿Cuándo llega el camión?
When does the truck arrive?
(guen das da trok a-*rraiv*)

¿Cuándo llegan los materiales?
When do the materials arrive?
(guen du da ma-*ti*-rials a-*rraiv*)

Necesito un nivel
I need a level.
(ai nid ei le-vel)

¿Dónde está?
Where is it?
(guer is et)

No está en el camión/ trailer.
It's not on the truck/ trailer.
(ets nat an da trok/ *trei*-ler)

¿Dónde ponemos lo extra?
Where do we put the extra?
(guer du ui put da ex-tra)

¿Quieres que limpie?
Do you want me to clean up?
(du iu guant mi tu clin ap)

¿Dónde nos lavamos?
Where do we clean ourselves up?
(guer du ui clin au-er-*selvs* ap)

¿Estás drogado/ borracho?
Are you stoned/ drunk?
(ar iu stond / drunk)

¿Podemos dejar las herramientas aquí?
Can we leave the tools here?
(can gui liv da *tuls* jir)

¿Me llevo el camión a casa?
Should I take a truck home?
(chud ai teik ei trok jom)

Adentro	Inside	*In-said*
Arbol	Tree	*Tri*
Área	Area	*Er-ia*
Abajo	Down	*Daun*
Abridor de hoyos	Aerator	*Er-ey-tor*
Abrir	Open	*O-pen*
Accidente	Accident	*Axi-dent*
Aceite	Oil	*Oil*
Acera	Sidewalk	*Said-walk*
Afuera	Outside	*Aut-said*
Agua	Water	*Ua-ter*
Aire	Air	*Ear*
Al lado	Next to	*Next tu*
Alambre	Wire	*Wair*
Almuerzo	Lunch break	*Lonch breik*
Alto	Stop	*Stap*
Alto	Tall	*Tol*
Antes de	Before	*Bi-for*
Anticongelante	Antifreeze	*Anti-friz*
Apagado	Off	*Of*
Aquí	Here	*Jir*
Arado	Plow	*Plau*
Arbustos	Bushes	*Bu-shes*
Arena	Sand	*Sand*
Arriba	Up	*Ap*
Aspersor	Sprinkler	*Sprin-kler*
Astártar	Choke	*Chok*
Atomizador	Sprayer	*Spre-yer*
Ayudar	Help	*Jelp*
Baja	Low	*Lou*
Baño	Bathroom	*Bath-rum*
Banderas	Flags	*Flags*
Barra	Bar	*Bar*
Barrer	Sweep	*Swip*
Barro	Mud	*Mad*
Bastante	Enough	*I-naf*
Basura	Trash	*Trash*

Basurero Dumpster *Dompster*
Bateri'a Battery *Ba-tery*
Bloque Block *Black*
Bolsa Bag *Bag*
Bomba Pump *Pamp*
Boquilla Nozzle *No-zol*
Borracho Drunk *Dronk*
Botas Boots *Buts*
Brocha de pintura Paint brush *Peint brosh*
Bueno Good *Gud*
Cabeza Head *Jed*
Cabeza de rotor Rotor head *Ro-tor jed*
Cadena Chain *Chein*
Caja Box *Box*
Caja de herramientas Tool box *Tul box*
Claiente Hot *Jat*
Calle Street *Strit*
Camino de entrada Driveway *Draiv-uey*
Cañeria del aqua Water main *Ua-ter mein*
Carretilla Wheel barrow *Gue'll barrou*
Césped Lawn *Lon*
Cemento Cement *Se-ment*
Cerca valla Fence *Fens*
Cerradura Lock *Lac*
Cerrar Close *Clos*
Cerveza Beer *Biir*
Chaqueta Jacket *Yaket*
Cincel Chisel *Chi-sol*
Cinta métrica Measuring tape *Me-shur-ing teip*
Cinta Tape *Teip*
Cinturón Belt *Belt*
Clavo Nail *Nail*
Co'mo How *Jau*
Compañia Company *Com-pa-ni*
Comprar Buy *Bilt*

Construir	Build	*Biold*
Correcto	Correct	*Co-rect*
Cortadora	Trimmer	*Tre-mer*
Cortadora de bordes	Edger	*Ed-yer*
Cortar	Cut	*Cat*
Cortar	Mow	*Mou*
Crudo	Hungover	*Hang-over*
Cuánto	How much	*Hau mach*
Cuarto de galón	Quart	*Cuart*
Cubeta/cubo	Bucket	*Ba-ket*
Cubrir	Mask	*Mask*
Cuchilla	Blade	*Bleid*
Cuchillo	Knife	*Naïf*
Cuerda	Rope	*Rop*
Cuerda de extensión	Extension cord	*Ex-ten-chon cord*
Cuidado	Careful	*Ker-ful*
Curbo	Curb	*Kurb*
Debajo	Below	*Bi-lou*
Debajo	Under	*An-der*
Dejar	Quit	*Cuit*
Derecho	Tight	*Rait*
Desafilado	Dull	*Dol*
Descargar	Unload	*An-load*
Después	After	*Af-ter*
Destornillador	Screwdriver	*Es-cru-drai-ver*
Detrás de	Behind	*Bi-haind*
Di'a de pago	Payday	*Pei-dei*
Dia libre	Day off	*Dei of*
Diferente	Different	*Di-fe-rent*
Dinero	Money	*Ma-ni*
Dirección	Direction	*Di-rec-chon*
Doler	Hurt	*Jort*
Duro	Hard	*Jard*
Electricidad	Electricity	*E-lek-tri-si ti*
Embarque	Clutch	*Clotch*
Embudo	Funnel	*Fanol*

Emergencia	Emergency	*E-mer-yen-si*
Empezar	Begin	*Bi-gin*
Empezar	Start	*Estart*
En	In	*In*
Encendido	On	*On*
Encima	Above	*Abov*
Enfermo	Sick	*Sik*
Enganchar	Coupler	*Kop-ler*
Equipo	Equipment	*I-cuip-ment*
Escalera	Ladder	*La-der*
Escalones	Stairs	*Esters*
Escavadora	Post hole digger	*Poust joul di'-ger*
Escoba	Broom	*Brum*
Esponja	Sponge	*Esponya*
Estacas	Stakes	*Esteiks*
Estuco	Stucco	*Estako*
Excavar	Dig	*Dig*
Fácil	Easy	*I-si*
Fertilizante	Fertilizer	*Fer-ti-lai-ser*
Filtro	Filter	*Fil-tur*
Filtro de gasolina	Fuel filter	*Gas fil-ter*
Flores	Flowers	*Flau-ers*
Freno	Brake	*Breik*
Frente	Front	*Frant*
Frió	Cold	*Kold*
Gafas de seguridad	Safety glasses	*Seif-ti glases*
Galo'n	Gallon	*Ga-lon*
Gasoline	Gas	*Gas*
Goma/rueda	Tire	*Tai-er*
Gotera	Leak	*Lik*
Gracias	Thank you	*Zaink-iu*
Grande	Big	*Big*
Grande	Large	*Larch*
Grapa	Staple	*Stei-pol*
Grava	Gravel	*Gra-vol*
Guantes	Gloves	*Glovs*

Hambre	Hungry	*Jan-gry*
Hojas	Leaves	*Livs*
Horca	Pitchfork	*Pitch-fork*
Hormigón/concreto	Concrete	*Can-crit*
Hoy	Today	*Tu-dei*
Hoyo	Hole	*Jol*
Insecticida	Insecticide	*In-sec-ti-said*
Invierno	Winter	*Gin-ter*
Irrigación	Irrigation	*I-rri-gei-chon*
Izquierdo	Left	*Left*
Jefe	Boss	*Bos*
La tarde	Afternoon	*After-nun*
Lado	Side	*Said*
Largo	Long	*Lang*
Lata	Can	*Can*
Lavar	Wash	*Guash*
Lechada	Grout	*Graut*
Lejos	Far	*Far*
Lesio’n/herida	Injury	*In-yuri*
Li’nea	Line	*Lain*
Libra	Pound	*Paund*
Libro	Book	*Buk*
Licencia	License	*Lai-sens*
Limpio	Clean	*Clin*
Linea primero	Main line	*Mein-lain*
Llata de gasoline	Gas can	*Gas can*
Llave inglesa	Wrench	*Rench*
Llaves	Keys	*Kis*
Lleno	Full	*Ful*
Lluvia	Rain	*Rein*
Lo seinto	Sorry	*Sarri*
Lona	Tarp	*Tarp*
Los partes	Fittings/parts	*Fi-tings/parts*
Máquina	Machine	*Ma-chin*
Madera	Wood	*Guud*
Major	Best	*Best*

Malas heirbas	Weeds	*Guids*
Malo	Bad	*Bad*
Mañana	Tomorrow	*Tu-ma-rrou*
Manguera	Hose	*Jous*
Mantenimiento	Maintenance	*Mein-te-nans*
Marcar	Mark	*Mark*
Martillo	Hammer	*Ja-mer*
Mas	More	*Mor*
Materiales	Materials	*Ma-ter-i-als*
Medio	Medium	*Mi-di-am*
Medio	Middle	*Mi-dol*
Menos	Less	*Les*
Metál	Metal	*Me-tal*
Milla	Mile	*Maiol*
Mirar	Look	*Luk*
Mismo	Same	*Seim*
Mojado	Wet	*Guet*
Mortero	Mortar	*Mor-ter*
Motor	Engine	*En-yin*
Motosierra	Chainsaw	*Chein-sa*
Moverse	Move	*Muv*
Mucho	A lot	*A lat*
Muchos	Many	*Meni*
Muro/pared	Wall	*Gual*
Necesito	Need	*Nid*
Nieve	Snow	*Esno'*
Ninguno	None	*Nan*
Nivelador	Level	*Le-vol*
Nivelar	Level	*Le-vol*
No se	I don't know	*Ai dount nou*
Norte	North	*Nortz*
Nuevo	New	*Niu*
Nunca	Never	*Ne-ver*
Officina	Office	*Af-is*
Otoño	Fall	*Fal*
Otra vez	Again	*Ag-en*
Paisaje	Landscape	*Land-eskeip*
Pala	Shovel	*Cha-vol*

Paleta	Trowel	*Trauel*
Parte	Part	*Part*
Pasto/hierba	Grass	*Gras*
Patio	Backyard	*Bak-iard*
Patio	Yard	*Iard*
Pedazo/pieza	Piece	*Pis*
Peligroso	Dangerous	*Dein-yer-as*
Pequen~o	Small	*Esmol*
Pesado	Heavy	*Jevy*
Pico	Pick axe	*Pik aks*
Pie	Foot	*Fut*
Piedra	Stone	*Eston*
Pintura	Paint	*Peint*
Pinzas/alicates	Pliers	*Play-ers*
Plástico	Plastic	*Plas-tic*
Plana	Plan	*Plan*
Planta	Plant	*Plant*
Planta perrene	Perrenial	*Per-en-ial*
Plantas annual	Annuals	*An-uals*
Podadera	Pruning shears	*Pru-ning chiars*
Poder	Can you	*Can-yu*
Poner	Put	*Put*
Por favor	Please	*Plis*
Porque	Because	*Bi-kas*
Pota carga	Forklift	*Fork-lift*
Poste	Post	*Post*
Preparado/listo	Ready	*Re-di*
Preparar	Prepare	*Pri-per*
Primavera	Spring	*Espring*
Primero	First	*Ferst*
Problema	Problem	*Prob-lem*
Profundo	Deep	*Dip*
Pulgada	Inch	*Inch*
Punto muerto	Neutral	*Niu-tral*
Qui'micos	Chemicals	*Ke-mi-cals*
Quitar	Remove	*Ri-muv*
Rajado	Craked	*Crakd*
Ramas	Branches	*Bran-chis*
Rápido	Hurry	*Jorry*

Rastrillo	Rake	*Reik*
Rela'mpago	Lightning	*Lait-ning*
Remolque	Trailer	*Trei-ler*
Ribete/borde	Edging	*Ed-ying*
Rincon	Corner	*Cor-ner*
Segadura	Lawnmower	*Lan-mo-er*
Semilla	Seed	*Sid*
Serrucho	Saw	*Sa'*
Siempre	Always	*Al-ueys*
Solicitud	Application	*a-pli-que-chon*
Sopladora	Blower	*Blo-uer*
Sueldo	Paycheck	*Pei-chek*
Suelo	Ground	*Graund*
Sujetar	Clamp	*Clamp*
Tabla	Board	*Bord*
También	Also	*Alsou*
Tanque de gasoline	Gas tank	*Gas tank*
Tarde	Late	*Leit*
Tela	Fabric	*Fa-bric*
Terminando	Done	*Dan*
Terrón	Sod	*Sad*
Tiempo parcial	Part time	*Par-taim*
Tienda	Shop	*Chap*
Tierra	Dirt	*Dert*
Tierra	Soil	*Soil*
Tiesto	Pot	*Pat*
Tijeras	Shears	*Chiars*
Tocón	Stump	*Estamp*
Todo	All	*Al*
Todo	Everything	*Evry-zing*
Tornillo	Screw	*Scru*
Trabajo	Jop	*Yab*
Trabajo	Work	*Uork*
Tractor	Tractor	*Trac-tor*
Trasera	Back	*Bak*
Tuberia	Pipe	*Paip*
Tubo blanco	P.V.C. pipe	*Pi-vi-si paip*

Tubo flexible	Swing pipe	*Suing paip*
Tubo Negro	Poly pipe	*Pali paip*
U'ltimo	Last	*Last*
Un poco	A little	*Ei litol*
Válvula	Valve	*Vealv*
Verano	Summer	*Sa-mer*
Viejo	Old	*Old*
Viento	Wind	*Guind*
Vivero	Nursery	*Ner-ser-i*
Yarda	Yard	*Ilard*
Zona	Zone	*Son*